COUPLE THERAPY:

Change Your Bad Habits in Love Following This Effective Couples Therapy Guide. You Can Easily Improve Your Marriage, Rescue Broken Relationship, Solve Most Common Conflicts.

By Michelle Miller

MICHELLE MILLER

© Copyright 2020 - All rights reserved.

The content contained within this book may not be reproduced, duplicated or transmitted without direct written permission from the author or the publisher.

Under no circumstances will any blame or legal responsibility be held against the publisher, or author, for any damages, reparation, or monetary loss due to the information contained within this book. Either directly or indirectly.

Legal Notice:

This book is copyright protected. This book is only for personal use. You cannot amend, distribute, sell, use, quote or paraphrase any part, or the content within this book, without the consent of the author or publisher.

Disclaimer Notice:

Please note the information contained within this document is for educational and entertainment purposes only. All effort has been executed to present accurate, up to date, and reliable, complete information. No warranties of any kind are declared or implied. Readers acknowledge that the author is not engaging in the rendering of legal, financial, medical or professional advice. The content within this book has been derived from various sources. Please consult a licensed professional before attempting any techniques outlined in this book.

By reading this document, the reader agrees that under no circumstances is the author responsible for any losses, direct or indirect, which are incurred as a result of the use of information contained within this document, including, but not limited to, — errors, omissions, or inaccuracies.

Table of Contents

Introduction 6

Chapter 1: Understand Each Partners Inner World 12

Chapter 2: Strengthen Friendship And Intimacy 17

Chapter 3: Finding Each Other In New Ways 24

Chapter 4: Facing The Future Together 26

Chapter 5: How Emotions Affect Your Partner 32

Chapter 6: Fighting Less And Feeling Better 40

Chapter 7: Protecting Your Relationship From Affairs 48

Chapter 8: Rescue Broken Relationship 54

Chapter 9: Some Example Of Conversation And Dialogue In Different Day Moments 58

Chapter 10: Significant Habits Of Good Relationships 64

Chapter 11: Cultivating New And Healthy Relationships 70

Chapter 12: How Do We Work Together 78

Chapter 13: Practice Empathy 84

Chapter 14: Couples And Compromise 90

Chapter 15: Know Your Partner 96

Chapter 16: Couples Therapy Exercises For Improving Communication 100

Chapter 17: Steps To Set Relationship Goals 106

Chapter 18: The Importance Of Having Fun To Couples 112

Chapter 19: Learn How To Apologize 119

Chapter 20: Accepting And Sharing Opinions 124

Chapter 21: How Couples Therapy Helps 130

Chapter 22: Things You Should Do Before Marriage 136

Chapter 23: Creating A Higher Sense Of Intimacy With Your Partner 142

Chapter 24: Marriage Secrets **148**
Chapter 25: Dealing With Temptations **154**
Chapter 26: How To Live A Happy Relationship **162**
Chapter 27: Overcoming Negative Thinking **170**
Chapter 28: Tips And Strategies To Maintain Your Emotional Wellbeing **178**
Chapter 29: How And Why To Protect Each Other **186**
Chapter 30: Love **194**
Conclusion **200**

MICHELLE MILLER

Introduction

Understanding of Couples therapy in all perspectives. You can also get the idea that how couples therapy work in the favor of couples. How couple therapy works as a beneficial source to reconnect couples and the whole phenomena behind it.

What is Couples therapy?

Counseling is for people who are married or are committed to each other. This is also referred to as a therapy for family. The purpose of couple therapy is to enhance and improve the relationship status of the couples. That form of counseling also help couples determine whether they should stay together or not. There are occasions when one or both parties need to discuss the psychological problems individually.

Understanding:

Therapy also involves sessions aimed at enhancing problem-solving, developing communication skills, and defining life goals and expectations for relationships. Many common problems include infidelity, financial difficulties, illness, and other changes in life, as well as frustration.

Counseling can be short-term or over a period of several months, depending on the extent of difficulties in relationship. If you and your wife are having problems because you end up in a big dispute any time you disagree, and fix absolutely nothing. The two of you are slowly growing apart due to the intense tension in the relationship. You have always thought about leaving your partner, but first, you want to try a couple therapy.

You are in counseling, and you understand that you both need guidance with the way you interact, and with your approach to problem-solving techniques. You also discover that you are simply continuing a form of behavior that was demonstrated by your parents: they yelled and accomplished nothing, and eventually fell apart and divorced. You can now change your actions with your newly gained awareness that part of the issue is that you follow what you have seen your parents do. You strengthen the relationship over time using constructive communication strategies and a workable issue solution. Positive feelings resurface for your partner, and you won't be able to believe that you had wanted to break the relationship.

Five Principles of Effective Couples therapy:

5 basic principles of effective couple's therapy are as follows:

1. Changes the views of the relationship:

Throughout the counseling process, the therapist tries to help both parties take a more realistic view of the relationship. They learn to avoid the "blame game" and look more at what happens to them in a cycle that includes both partner. You may also benefit from ensuring that their relationship exists in a specific context. For instance, couples who struggle financially may be put under different forms of situational stress than those who do not. Therapists begin this process by gathering "evidence" about the partners 'relationship by observing how they communicate. Therapists then formulate "hypotheses" about what factors could contribute to the problems in their relationship between the partners. Therapists share the knowledge with the couple according to the basic psychological perspective of the therapist and it also varies from couple to couple. With a range of methods, from clinical to insight-oriented, there is empirical support. Different therapists can use various approaches, but as long as they work on improving the perception of the relationship, the couple will begin to see each other and their experiences in a more constructive way.

2. Modifies dysfunctional behavior:

Good couple therapists try to improve the way the partners actually communicate with one another. In addition to helping them enhance their relationship, this means that therapists do need to ensure that their clients do not participate in behaviors that can cause physical, psychological, or economic damage. To do so, therapists must carry out a detailed evaluation to decide if their clients are genuinely at risk. For example, if possible, the therapist may recommend that one person be sent to a shelter for domestic violence, a specialist clinic for substance abuse, or anger management. It is also likely that if the risk isn't serious enough, the couple can benefit from "time-out" measures to avoid conflict escalation.

3. Decreases emotional avoidance:

Couples that refrain from sharing their private feelings are at greater risk of being emotionally isolated and growing apart. Efficient couple therapists help their clients put out the feelings and ideas they are unable to convey to others. Couple counseling based on intimacy helps couples to feel less anxious to communicate their desire for closeness. According to this view, some partners in childhood who have failed to build "free" emotional attachments have unmet needs that they bring into their adult relationships. They are afraid to show their partners how much they need them because they are afraid their partners are going to reject them. Behavioral therapists believe that adults may be unable to communicate their true feelings because they have not received "reinforcement" in the past. Either way, all psychological strategies recommend encouraging their clients to convey their true feelings in a way that would ultimately bring them back together.

4. Improves communication:

Intimacy is one of the "three C's" of being able to communicate. All positive couple therapies are geared towards helping the couples connect more effectively. Building on concepts 2 and 3, this contact should not be violent, nor will partners make one another crazy as they share their true feelings. Therefore, couples can need "coaching" in order to learn to talk to one another in a more supportive and understanding way. The therapist can also give instructional advice to the couple and provide them with the basis for understanding what forms of communication are successful and what forms would only create more tension. For example, they could learn how to listen more actively and empathetically. Just how to achieve this step, however, allows therapists to switch back to the tests they carried out early in care. Couples with a persistent history of mutual criticism can involve an approach different from those who seek to avoid confrontation at all costs.

5. Promote strengths:

Good couple therapists point out the strengths of the relationship and develop resilience, particularly when therapy is about to end. Since so much couple counseling includes concentrating on problem areas, it's easy to lose sight of the other areas where couple work effectively. Promoting strength is about helping the couple gain more satisfaction from their relationship. The behaviorally focused therapist can "prescribe" one partner to do something agreeable to another. Perhaps therapists from other orientations who concentrate more on feelings may help the couple create a more optimistic "plot" or narrative about their relationship. In this case, the therapist should stop trying to put his or her own perspective on what constitutes a strength and let the couple determine this.

We can see, then, that if their life seems hopeless, people in strained relationships need not give up in despair. In the same way, people who are reluctant to enter into long-term relationships will be motivated to learn how to repair problem relationships.

Looking at the other side, these five concepts of good counseling recommend strategies for partners to develop healthy close relationships and sustain them. Take an unbiased look at your relationship, seek assistance in eliminating unhealthy habits, feel like you can express your feelings, connect openly, and show what works. Most importantly, by ensuring that each partnership has its own specific challenges and strengths, you can give yours the best survival chances.

How does Couple therapy work?

Counseling will benefit couples with the use of the above approaches and more. For couple counseling to succeed, both people must be committed to enhancing their partnership while looking inwardly at their own strengths and weaknesses. Knowing their behaviors and habits that make your partner tick could have a positive impact on making improvements in both personal aspect and relationships. Couple's therapy is not intended to unload anger, frustration, and other negative actions against one spouse. It's about finding passion, commitment, and all the other approaches that lead a healthy relationship.

Does Marriage Counseling Work? That's a very big issue, but what people are really talking about is, "Will marriage therapy save my marriage? The response to that is very much based on a variety of variables beyond the counselor's office.

Although some of these points are highlighted below, some of the considerations to look for when seeking marital therapy are as follows:

1. Did you just wait too long? If you have been breaking each other apart for ten years, there is a very good risk that there is so much harm that it cannot be done to undo.

2. Need to save your marriage, really? People often go to therapy just to claim they've tried. They just don't want it to work. They save face just to assuage their remorse.

3. Is there harassment or aggression in the relationship? If there is a family, you're not trying to save it; you're trying to avoid the illegal activity. Abusers, whether physical or mental, are not "unhappy" in their marriage; they are often terrified and impotent people who feel helpless in their lives anywhere else.

4. Will the structure meet your needs? If saving your marriage means spending another 30 years doing away with everything you want to do, is that worth it? It takes a hard and truthful look at what every person needs to make sure you get exactly that what you need out of the relationship.

One of the most important factors in relationship counseling's success is the counselor. Nearly every counselor in the world claims they're doing marital therapy, but most never received any preparation. They also have a psychology or counseling degree and believe they should do it.

CHAPTER 1:

Understand Each Partners Inner World

When we are in a relationship, we desire to be heard, seen and understood. Understanding the other person is as important as being understood. We want to know that "we are being listened to, we are being understood". In fact, we want our spouse to say "Yes I hear you, yes I understand and yes I feel your pain. I am sorry that it hurts and know that I will be here for you." We desire that our partners are interested in us and what we are going through. These desires are basic human needs.

One of the key complaints raised by people in conflict is that they are not feeling understood or cared for. Feeling unheard, unseen and misunderstood is a killer of intimacy. if we do not feel understood, we feel rejected, more like it does matter. That will hinder relational growth and lead to fractures in the relationship in due time.

Being understanding is listed among the top qualities that facilitate a good relationship. Apart from allowing your partner to be him/herself in the relationship, it lets you see things from the perspective of other people without fear of being vulnerable. Most of us strive to be understanding to our partners.

There is an inaccurate belief that understanding a partner means that one has to agree with him/her. That is not true. You can understand someone and still disagree with him/her. Understanding simply means that you are listening to your partner objectively. It involves listening intently and fully to all the opinions of the other person and actually understood without interfering with your own opinions and judgments. In fact, you can check that what you heard is right by rephrasing the words of the partner. For instance, you can say, "I understand what you are saying but let me check, what you are saying is..."

Such fact-checking will reassure your partner that you are listening, understanding and also staying in touch with their words. Make sure that your partner feels so understood that he sees no reason to keep clarifying his/her perspective. Below are some of the procedures you can use to understand your partner better.

a. Understand first

When having a conversation, you do not have to give your opinion first. In fact, you do not have to start thinking of a solution before the person has finished talking. In most cases, our ability to understand something is affected by the thoughts running through our heads because we start thinking of a solution as soon as the other person starts to talk. Your main role in a conversation is to be a listening human being to your partner first. Be the pillar and shoulder they need. No matter how much you feel like sharing your opinion, reserve it. If your partner feels fully understood, he/she will reciprocate by giving you full attention and trying to understand your feelings, thoughts and perceptions.

b. Be fully present

Sometimes during a conversation, we are distracted by things such as our own thoughts, perceptions and even stresses. This only hinders us from understanding the other person fully. Be fully present. You can even use active listening skills to minimize the degree of distraction. You too will want to be understood fully when it is your turn to talk.

c. Avoid defensiveness and complaints

Complains are very toxic and defensiveness prevents us from truly understanding the perspectives of other people. In most cases, we avoid being vulnerable by being defensive. Intimacy requires openness and vulnerability. To avoid pushing your partner to the defense, do not use critiques. Instead of pointing out their mistakes aggressively, use the 'I statement' to explain how you felt. If you keep pointing at the faults of your partner, you are simply saying "It is your fault, not mine."

The trick to making sure that your partner feels understood is taking some of the blame. By sharing responsibility, you leave room for expression. You can say something positive like "I know I said …. And failed but …." It is also very important to tell your partner about your feelings and needs.

d. Understand yourself

If a person commits into a relationship without understanding his/herself first, it might brew trouble. Basically, before you start to involve another person in your problems, make sure that you know them yourself. That way, you will know what is bothering you at any one point.

It is very hard to help another person while we are burdened by our own problems. You will have trouble managing all the problems bubbling up in a relationship if you do not even know what is prickling at your heart. As such, it is very important to take some time and connect with yourself, connect with your feeling and acknowledge your emotions.

If you feel there are needs you need to heal in yourself, explain this to your partner. You can say "I want to understand you but first, I need some time with myself. Can you allow me time? That will make your partner to feel that you are trying and not being just selfish.

To understand yourself, tune in to your thoughts, feelings, and bodily sensations. This will help you to identify the things happening to you, which can be shared with your partner. Some of the physical signs that might help you understand yourself include, a racing heart, hair prickling up, the sensation in your mind, et cetera. Understanding a person requires patience. It means not interrupting our partners. It means listening without formulating premature responses. Understanding requires one to turn the full attention towards the other person. This is not easy, especially when you have personal baggage.

Understanding a person requires practice. Be patient and give your partner the special gift of being seen, heard and understood.

e. Do not impose your own beliefs and ideas

Regardless of the amount of experience, knowledge, maturity, and intellect you have, never impose ideas on your partner. Technically, this self-imposition feels like intimidation to a loved one. Doing this will hinder you from truly understanding the feelings of your partner.

To be an understating partner in a relationship, you need to acknowledge that no matter how much you know, your partner has his/her personality. He/she has ideas, feelings, thoughts, knowledge and beliefs. And you have to know and respect them even if you do not agree with them. This is necessary to keep a strong bond.

f. Allow your partner to live

Sometimes, we want our partner to leave everything else and live with us, that is, make the relationship the only thing in his/her life. In fact, many people crave to be the center of their partner's universe. Here is the thing, it is possible to have a partner make you the center of his/her world but, that will not last. Do not force your partner to drop most of their life choices and preferences for the relationship.

Ensure that you understand your partner and give him/she the freedom to have fun, just live, and enjoy life even without you. Besides, you need to respect your partner as a social being. It is unhealthy and selfish to limit your partner just because you are in a relationship. Let him/her go out with associates, spend time with family, travel on his/her own and live life to the fullest without your interference. Above all, let your partner pursue his/her goals and offer support.

CHAPTER 2:

Strengthen Friendship and Intimacy

1. Start Trusting

Learn to get into the habit of trusting people more consciously. Choose a trusting disposition over a distrustful attitude. Unless you have concrete evidence about someone, take their word for it. Going around snooping, stalking your partner and behaving like a suspicious maniac only harms your relationship further. Rather, if there is no reason to be suspicious other than a feeling of insecurity or jealously, let it go.

2. Write Your Deepest Feelings and Thoughts

Journaling is well-known to be one of the most effective techniques for bringing to the fore your deepest feelings and emotions. It helps you discover multiple layers of your personality to achieve greater self-awareness. It also facilitates the process of an emotional catharsis for venting out pent up feelings. For instance, you may constantly harbor feelings of insecurity because neglectful parents raised you or you may never feel you are "good enough" because you were raised by parents who had extremely high and unreasonable expectations from you.

People who have been wronged in their childhood often feel they aren't worthy enough to be loved. This in turn causes them to reflect that their partner is seeking someone more worthy or deserving of love than them, which creates feelings of insecurity.

3. Regulate Your Negative Feelings and Emotions with Mindfulness

Mindfulness is a great way to calm your nerves and manage runaway emotions. Tune into your physical and mental self by identifying your feelings, thoughts and emotions by taking deep breaths. Try and detach yourself from overpowering negative emotions such as jealousy and insecurity. Every time you find yourself overcome with thoughts of jealousy or insecurity, practice mindful meditation.

4. Be Frank and Accepting About Your Feelings

Discussing your insecurities with your partner will help you create a frank and open communication channel. Rather than doing and saying crazy things to your partner, be upfront and share your feelings. Say something similar to "I apologize for bothering you regarding your friendship with ABC, but it is not my lack of trust in you. I simply feel insecure about it."

5. Avoid Suffocating Your Partner

Start relaxing a bit by letting go of your desire to imprison your partner. The harder you try to imprison someone against his/her own will, the more forcefully they'll try to escape your domineering behavior. Let your partner have the choice to spend time with his/her friends, talk to their attractive colleague or do other things that otherwise make you feel threatened. Once they realize how secure and confident you are about the relationship, they will automatically be drawn to you. A secure and self-assured partner can be extremely irresistible.

6. Create Boundaries as a Couple

Sometimes people act in a certain way without even being aware that their actions negatively impact loved ones. You may find your partner indulging in flirtatious behavior often, but he/she may believe it to be a part of their fun personality. They may not even be aware of the damage being caused to you or the relationship. For them it may be a harmless display of their charm and wit.

Setting boundaries early in the relationship will keep you both on the same page as to what is appropriate or acceptable behavior and where to draw the line. You both can mutually discuss and arrive at the "non-negotiable" in your relationship. Is harmless flirting alright with both of you? What about kissing on the cheek? Dancing with a member of the opposite sex? Once clear boundaries are established, your partner will be less likely to behave in a way that can upset your or incite feelings of insecurity. Talk issues through, look for a common ground and once everything is clear – learn to trust your partner unless there is compelling evidence to believe otherwise.

7. Go to the Bottom of Your Insecurity and Negative Emotions

It can be really hard to objective assess why you feel pangs of insecurity each time someone compliments your partner, or he/she speaks warmly with his/her colleagues. It can be highly tempting to blame another person for your emotions. However, getting to the root of your insecurity by being more self-aware is the foundation to free yourself from its shackles. Take a more compassionate and objective look at the origination of your insecurity. Think about the potential causes for feelings of insecure.

For instance, if you find yourself being increasingly insecure of your partner, know why you feel it. Is it because you don't want to lose him/her? Do you agonize from a false sense of self-entitlement that your partner's time belongs only to you? Do you feel what you feel because of a sense of inadequacy that constantly makes you think "you aren't good enough?" Once you identify the underlying reasons causing feelings of jealousy and insecurity, it becomes easier to deal with your behavior.

8. Switch Off from Envious and Insecure Mental Chatter

Tell yourself to mentally shut up when you find yourself engaging in self-defeating jealous self-speak. You can use several ways to achieve this. It can be using a stop or "x" sign whenever negative thoughts begin to pick momentum in your mind. Condition yourself to stop unexpected thoughts with practice sessions using visual and mental reinforcements. Try saying stop aloud when you find yourself embarking on a destructive insecurity self-talk journey. This way you will embarrass yourself more and realize how ridiculously you are behaving. The idea is to train your mind into thinking that it isn't alright to come up with insecure self-talk.

9. Avoid Judging Other People Based on Your Past

Ever notice how suspicious people are always suspicious of others? Or liars think everyone around them is lying? Our perception of people and their motives is often a reflection of who we are. Stop using your past or present behavior as a yardstick for perceiving your partner's actions. For instance, if you have a history of being involved with married men/women, do not assume that no married man/woman can ever be trusted and start mistrusting your spouse. Just because you did or are doing something does not mean he/she is indulging in it too.

10. Discard past Relationship Baggage

A strong reason why you are always paranoid about your current partner cheating on you can be traced back to an earlier relationship. You may have had an ex-partner cheat on you with your best friend. The betrayal may have had such a severe impact that you view every relationship in a similar distrustful light.

Painting everyone with the same brush can be a disastrous mistake in any relationship. There is a solid reason your earlier relationship did not last, and you should leave the garbage of your earlier relationship where it belongs – in the trash can.

11. Question Yourself Every Time

Each time you find yourself feeling even remotely jealous; question the underlying feeling behind the complex emotion of jealousy. Is the insecurity a consequence of my anger, anxiety or fear? What is it about this circumstances that makes me jealous? When you question your jealously critically, you are a few steps away from taking constructive steps to convert a cloud of negativity into a bundle of positivity.

12. Insecurity Is Not Always an Evil Monster

It may sound contradictory to everything we've been discussing about insecurity, but truth is insecurity may not always be harmful. Sometimes, a tiny amount of it may do your relationship a whole lot of good. How? It can sometimes motivate you or your partner to safeguard your relationship. If expressed in a productive and wholesome manner, insecurity gives you the much-needed impetus to protect your territory. Insecurity helps you assume the role of a protector for your loved one and relationship, and this can be good if it doesn't scale extreme heights. Be smart enough to realize when jealousy goes from being a relationship protector to a relationship destroyer. You choose whether it is a boon or bane for your relationship.

13. Remind Yourself of Your Strengths Periodically

Each of us possesses unique strengths that set us apart from others. Keep reinforcing to yourself how wonderful you are through positive affirmations and visualizations. You will find yourself feeling less insecure when you are aware of your positives. The more self-assured and confident you are, the less affected you will be by other people's actions. Know where your strengths lie, keep doing things that make you feel great about yourself and believe that you are worthy of true love.

14. Focus on Productive and Positive Ideas

Rather than obsessing over who your partner is cheating you with, try to develop interests outside of your relationship. Do not make it the nucleus of your existence even if it means a lot to you.

15. Imaginary Fears Do Not Necessarily Mean It Will Happen

We need to understand that our insecure hunches do not necessarily mean the act is occurring. Just because we fear something is going to happen doesn't mean it will happen. A majority of the times our fears are unfounded, and not even remotely close to coming true. Just because your partner is somewhere else, and you fear he/she is with someone else doesn't mean he/she is proposing relationship on a date. Understand the difference between thoughts and actual events. The make-believe imaginations of our destructive mind are often far from reality.

16. Be Generous

Spend more time giving and helping others. This will not just make you feel great about yourself but also help you develop a greater understanding of how you add value to others' lives and how they would be grateful to have what you have.

Volunteer within your local community by helping folks read and write English or preparing meals for the less fortunate or even assisting a friend who is struggling to finish college.

17. Stay Away from Insecurity Triggering Situations

Be aware of situations that trigger elements of jealousy and insecurity in your behavior and avoid these situations whenever you can. For instance, if you are a person who can't help experiencing pangs of insecurity each time your partner mingles with members of the opposite sex, avoid dating a person who generally hangs out with the opposite sex and is extremely popular with them. This will invariably lead to friction unless you work a common ground.

18. Focus on the Positives

So, you witnessed your partner flirting with one of his friends. Big deal? Not really. Keep in mind that you both have a history of intimacy and an incomparable closeness, which is why you are together in the first place. There's a unique spark about your togetherness that cannot be matched by others. Just because someone pays their friends a few compliments and displays warmth doesn't necessarily mean they want to be with him/her for life. Sometimes, people just flirt to lighten the mood or break the ice or make the other person feel good about himself/herself.

Remember the really positive and unusual things about your relationship every time you are overcome with feelings of insecurity/jealousy. Remind yourself of your beautiful moments, of everything your partner has told you about why he/she fell in love with you, and the loving things you have done for each other.

CHAPTER 3:

Finding Each Other In New Ways

It's quick to get in a rut and continue to feel isolated from each other in these days of tight budgets, long working days, and jobs that keep us apart. Here are six separate ways you can make minimal effort or money every day that mutually influence your partner's attitude and can help to rekindle the spark in your relationship. The following list will help control your partner's opinion and keep him or her talking about you all day. This is such that the day to day they face their work doesn't preclude them from spending a beautiful night together when they get home.

- Tomorrow, add a cup of coffee and tea to your partner's room. There's no need to have just a hot meal. Easy toast or coffee cereal is the work.
- Ask them as you go, about how wonderful their companion feels, or how fine their hair or wardrobe looks today.
- Call your companion during the day just to let them know your feelings about them. Should not lament or say anything. Don't worry. Keep that for friends. Leave that for children. Depending on the work of your friend, you might need to be imaginative to find the right way to communicate without competing with your job. Two options to do that are to post messages to your personal cell phone, to immediately send an e-mail and, of course, to a fast phone call.
- If it is possible to meet your friend for lunch at least once a week.

- The minute you first see each other in the afternoon or after work, just hug them, kiss them, and tell them if you missed them before you say something.
- Seek not to get into a rut in the evening. Any night, mix up what you do. One night I go for dinner, rent a movie for one night, go for a walk, meet friends for one night and play the game for the weekend. Too many couples do their own thing every night in a rut of the same routine. Often work has to be done and time allocated to the task of making a living, but I believe you ought to diversify your post-work routine in order to avoid forming poor habits that mess with your connection. If you follow the above list sincerely and do it over and over for a long time, I guarantee that your relationship will start to feel different again.
- You both discover something entirely new for all of you is like joining unfamiliar waters together. In other words, this is an experience that almost always leads to pleasure, excitement, and laughter. If you pick a class where both of you are novices, you can, of course, rely on each other to find out details. Best of all, once you're doing it, you'll be "experts," you will have opportunities to talk about each other, your kids, and your social network.
- Record Your Happiness thought of the last shot you and your friend have shared together. When your relationship is ten years old, the latest proof, it is time to create new memories and record them. Take a mirror to your study; take brochures of the school. Save all the sheets of directions as well as other souvenirs. Using them to build a beautiful scrapbook for you and your friend. This is a perfect way to honor each other's new engagement.

CHAPTER 4:

Facing the Future Together

If you want your marriage to last a lifetime, you need to build your future together. Often, we come across couples who are so disconnected they hardly know what is going on in each other's lives. Staying invested in each other's goals, happiness, and dreams will keep you connected and reaching for the same future. When you are able to create a shared vision for your marriage it is easy to stay on track because you have a clear idea of what you are both aiming for.

Your spouse needs to be more than just someone you share a house or children with. You need to be partners in life. This means that even when you both have different passions and dreams your goals are aligned and you are working to achieving the same goals. You need to plan your future together so that you can work together to make it a reality.

One of the signs in any relationship is when you and your spouse do not talk about the future. When you have no idea of what you want your future to look like as a couple, it means that you are not really invested in that relationship. There is no guarantee that your marriage will last forever but if you are genuinely invested in your relationship you will have plans for the future.

The plans that you make will set the tone for your marriage and determine how you evolve both as individuals and as partners in a relationship. There is also a sense of stability and security that comes with knowing that you are building a future together. This security fosters trust and enables you to stay connected to your partner in the long term.

Strategies for building your future together

1. Be open about finances

In any marriage, your attitudes towards money will impact both of your futures. That is why having a conversation about money is crucial when trying to plan for your future. Conflicts about money are frequent in many marriages and the only way to get around this is to have a financial plan.

Agree on household budgets, saving plans, and your expenditure. This helps to lay down guidelines that both of you can live by in order to achieve your financial goals. A solid business plan helps to secure you a comfortable future and free you from constant financial worries.

If necessary, you can consult a professional to help you come up with a financial plan that works for both you and your partner. Being able to agree on money matters reduces conflict in your relationship and fosters trust.

2. Share responsibilities

A marriage is a partnership and this means you should be willing to share responsibilities. From house chores to parenting duties and all the commitments that come with running a family, sharing responsibilities creates a healthy balance in the relationship.

Sharing responsibilities will help to prevent the resentment that starts to creep up in relationships when one person feels like they are being taken advantage of. Come up with a list of duties and responsibilities and agree who is tasked with what. Of course, the duties can be switched between partners if need be but assigning creates some accountability in the marriage.

3) Build trust in your relationship

By being open and honest with each other about your goals, needs, and dreams, you can create trust in the relationship and forge stronger bonds. It is reassuring to know what your spouse is working toward and the things that are most important to them.

Being upfront about your expectations of each other will also help to avoid any feelings of disillusionment down the line. Do not keep your spouse in the dark about the things that you are planning for your future. When you know each other's plans, you can support each other and understand where you are both coming from as well as what your aspirations are.

4) Have fun together

Do not let your relationship become a dull affair. Inject some fun and romance by finding fun things to go together. Sign up for a dancing class, visit new places, or just find hobbies that appeal to you both. Spending time bonding and having fun helps to relieve pressure and build intimacy.

If you have date nights, make them fun by doing something different every time. Keeping things light-hearted and fun shows your partner that you can keep the relationship exciting and exciting. Being spontaneous and adventurous will help to keep your marriage feeling young no matter how old you are.

Remember just because you have been together for long, you do not have to turn into an old boring couple.

5) Give your partner space from time to time

Creating freedom in your relationship is excellent for ensuring the longevity of your marriage. Do not make your partner feel like you want to control them and monitor them all the time.

Have enough independence to give your partner space and room to breathe.

Giving each other space shows that you trust each other and that you are secure in your relationship. When your partner feels they still have the freedom to be themselves and pursue their passions, they will not be anxious about spending the rest of their life with you.

6) Embrace your differences

If you actually want to be together forever, you need to accept and embrace each other's differences. Stop the constant criticizing and judging. People want to know that their partner takes them, warts and all, in order to feel comfortable planning a future together.

When you feel tempted to attack or find fault in your partner, remember the bigger picture and consider whether you want to build animosity or intimacy. No matter who you end up with, there will always be things you differ on. Part of being emotionally intelligent is having enough self-awareness to accept not just yourself but your spouse.

There is no such thing as a perfect marriage, but with the right attitude and relationship skills, you can create a beautiful life for you and your spouse.

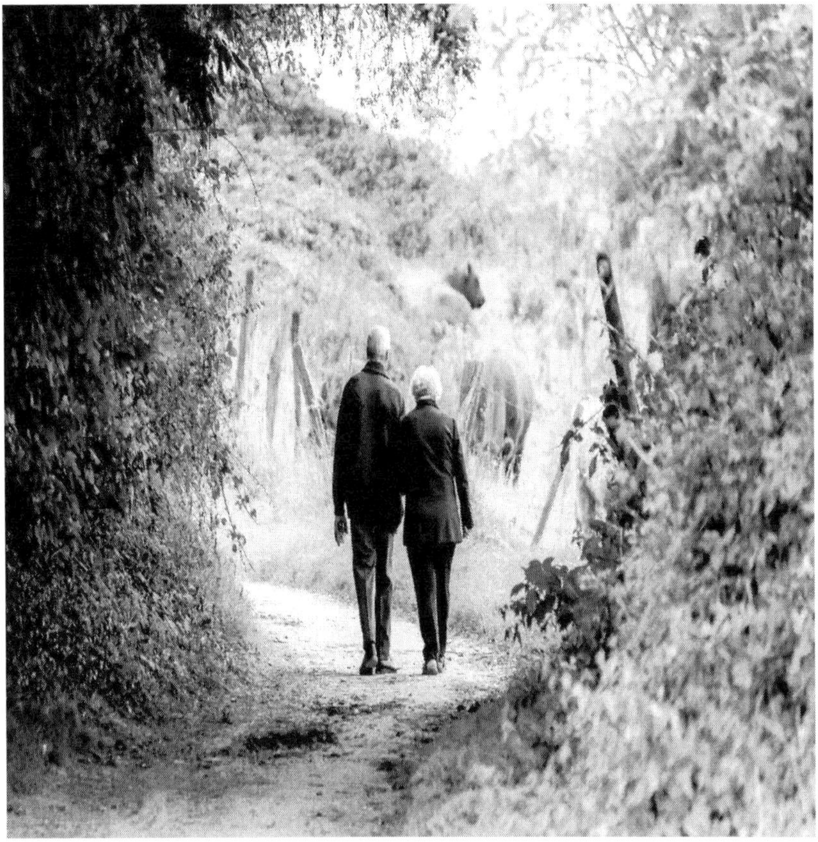

CHAPTER 5:

How Emotions Affect Your Partner

Anger is a normal human emotion but a powerful one for that matter. It is essential to show frustration, hurt, disappointment, and annoyance with other people, including romantic partners. It is healthy for you to express anger when aggrieved by your partner, but you should do it in a controlled way.

When you express anger in unhealthy ways, you not only hurt your partner, but you also prevent yourself from conveying what exactly your problem with the situation you are in is. When you express anger in unhealthy ways, you also damage your relationship and make it impossible to salvage the once healthy, loving relationship you had with your partner.

Unmanaged anger also interferes with the quality of life that you lead as it affects your physical and mental health. To avoid all this, people can learn to control their anger. It is possible to manage anger in healthier ways. Here are a few ways to do so.

Once you're Calm, Express Your Anger

When your partner aggrieves you, it is crucial for you to let your anger subside before confronting him or her. This ensures that you do not say something that you cannot take back in the heat of an argument. If you cannot get away, try taking some deep breaths before you speak to the person.

Once you have your emotions under control, try to pinpoint exactly why you are upset or what exactly has set off the feelings that you are feeling. There are times when people get irritable because of other things that are happening in their lives.

You can begin by first telling the other person how difficult the situation is for you. By doing this, you disarm them and force them to show you empathy, which means that they also get distracted and forget about their anger.

Once both of you are calm, you can continue to explain the reason why you are upset and convey precisely what you are mad about. In the process, you should also talk about the emotions that you are feeling and how the other person's actions affect you. You should also focus on the current problem and not what mistakes your partner did in the past. If you, at any point, sense that your anger is beginning to rise, take a break. This gives you time to cool down and gather back your thoughts. You can also try counting one to ten as you practice some heavy breathing.

As you speak, be assertive but not hostile. Assertive communication involves stating only that which is factual without pointing accusations at the other person. As you point out an issue or issues, do not talk in a confrontational way, this can agitate the other party and cause them to react in anger. When you speak while calm, the other person is also able to listen and understand what you are saying.

Once you finish giving all your concerns, you should also provide the other party the same opportunity to state their case and the reason behind their actions. Try to see things from their perspective before you react in any way. Both of you should listen to one another keenly and repeat what you think the person means to gain a better understanding of each other.

Take A Timeout

Anger clouds people's judgment, so it is always a good idea to take time out of a confrontational situation to calm down. Timeout also gives the other person the same space to thinks about the issue at hand. Depending on the problem, the timeout can be as brief as a few minutes or can last even a few days. In a short timeout, people can practice some quick relaxing techniques. Some quiet time away, even in front of your partner, can give both of you time to cool down.

Counting to 100 can also help to take your mind off the situation and reset. After the timeout, you can begin to gather your thoughts calmly again. Anytime you sense like you are about to explode, you can get away and take a short walk outside or around the block to clear your head.

Exercise is also an excellent way to blow off steam. You can choose to go for a run or have an intense work out session at the gym. A high-energy consuming activity like boxing or martial arts, will distract and exhaust you to the point that you forget about your problem for a while.

Breathing exercises can also be beneficial, especially if coupled with an activity like yoga. However, you should look for something that you enjoy doing which you know can relax you.

You can also talk to a third party to vent out your anger and the frustrations you are undergoing in your relationship. This person can simply lend a listening ear, but they can also give a better perspective of the situation and reaffirm or try to change your perception of the case. The person can also help you to identify the exact cause of your feelings clearly.

Any activity that works to distract or calm you down like a shower, writing, listening to music is also worth a try.

Identify Possible Solutions

As you try to work out your issues with your partner, look for solutions to your problem instead of dwelling on the problem. If you find yourself always getting irritated with your partner because of a particular habit or situation, remove yourself from the trigger. Getting upset all the time does not help in dealing with life's frustrations.

You can decide to change your reaction towards other people's actions and in this case, your partner. Challenge your thinking and get down to the root cause of your anger. Identify the thought patterns that lead you to violence and change them. Make a decision to let go of situations that you cannot control as well as angry thoughts. You can also try to develop resilience in conditions that have the potential of making you angry.

Taking care of both your psychological and physical health on a daily basis also ensures that you are able to deal with people in the right way. People who are always stressed find themselves getting angry too often and too quickly. Daily exercises, even for a few minutes in a day, can help relax your body and burn out any stress that you might be experiencing. Meditation and deep breathing exercises also help in relaxing your body. Taking breaks to go for a holiday or enjoy a day out can help relax your mind.

Quality sleep also gives your body time to relax and rejuvenate in order to be able to handle any stressors or challenges that come your way. Experts advocate for at least 8 hours of sleep on a daily basis. Substance use and alcohol consumption also impair a person's ability to make sound decisions and reason, therefore avoid them if you can. You should also keep the consumption of high-energy drinks and caffeine at minimum levels to avoid being irritable.

Self-help books and self-help programs can also teach you anger management skills as well as healthier ways of expressing anger.

If you still find yourself incapable to control your anger with any of the above techniques and you keeping hurting your significant other, you can enroll for anger management classes to help you cope with your anger issues. Such levels advise and teach you healthier ways of managing your anger. Depending on how out of control your passion is, you can sign up for a one-off class, a weekend program, or a one-month program. Until you are able to manage your anger, you should seek all the possible help you can get.

Therapy is also an option. Psychologists can help people deal with other underlying issues that may contribute to them always feeling angry.

Do Not Hold a Grudge

Once you and your partner address a particular issue, you should close that chapter and move on. If you cannot agree with your partner, you can always agree to disagree and move on with life. You can also decide to ignore your partner's shortcomings and find a way of living with them. Another way to distract yourself is to focus on the good qualities your partner has. This takes your mind off things that irritate you.

Whatever way you choose to take, you should not keep dwelling on past issues, and neither should you keep bringing up past mistakes in future conversations or arguments with your partner. Holding grudges and reminding each other of one another's errors or listing each other wrongdoings will only escalate anger.

You should also practice forgiveness. Forgiveness has the power to heal you as well as the other party. When you forgive a person, they are likely to become conscious of their mistakes, and this can lead them to make a point of never repeating them again. Forgiveness also makes both parties let go of any negative feeling that they may have, which gives room for the healing process to begin.

Agreeing on healthy ways to resolve issues in your relationship also prevents couples from going at each other in the future. Couples should even know the difference between letting things go and suppressing their anger. Repressing anger is unhealthy in relationships. If you still feel resentment towards your partner, then chances are you are controlling some issues with your partner, and you need to be open about them to avoid exploding at your partner in the future.

Holding on to anger also affects the quality of life that you live and interferes with your physical, mental health, and overall well-being. Constant anger floods your body with stress hormones that increase heart rate and blood pressure. With time, recurrent passion can lead to heart disease, stroke, and psychological disorders.

Use Humor to Release Tension

You can use humor to change the mood in an otherwise tense room, but you should use it creatively, or it can end up doing more harm than good. You should never laugh at the other person's mistakes, their weakness, or their lack of sound judgment. Do not insult their intelligence or way of thinking. The other party may become upset and make a regrettable statement, which will only fuel the anger that both of you are currently dealing with.

You should avoid sarcasm or bad jokes that are insulting. Instead, try to direct most of the fun at yourself or at the situation. Self-deprecating humor, when dealing with anger, is used to remind the other people that everyone has flaws and can make mistakes, so they should not feel too bad about their wrongdoings.

When you use humor well, it can disarm the other party and bring his or her defenses down. Humor also prevents the two parties from hurting each other's feelings. It also reduces any tension between the two people, which creates a situation where both parties can begin to discuss the issue at hand and come to an agreement.

Silent humor can also help you cope with your anger. For example, you can draw a mental picture of your partner as a tiny mischievous cartoon devil with horns. You can choose to share the image with your partner or not, but in either case, the funny cartoon image can help distract you from your anger.

CHAPTER 6:

Fighting Less and Feeling Better

Ups and downs are part of relationship. Where there is love, there are conflicts, disagreement, and miscommunication as well. To minimize such events, try to avoid conflicts and do everything to gain your partner's love and attention. By doing so, you tend to bottle up your feelings and needs.

In this process, the bottle becomes full, and you realize that you are the only one in your relationship who is putting all the efforts to make the link right. When you feel alone and taken for granted, you will experience the hurt and tend to feel angry with your partner. This pattern will lead to more adverse circumstances and cannot make you happy. There is a better way for you to adopt.

With the help of compassionate self-awareness, you will be able to tolerate your emotions and learn to value yourself. You will become a positive person and will be able to take positive feedback from the caring and loving people in your life.

Consequently, you will be able to ignore the negative energy and will focus on the positive aspects of the relationship. This will help to maintain an intimate relationship with your partner. When you are expressive in a positive and enjoyable way, then healthy relationships are maintained. You will be able to know the coping mechanism to deal with the conflicts you face in the relationship.

Practices for support

Asking for support is the approach that helps to nurture the relationship. Asking what you want and need in a relationship helps to make the relationship stronger. Two basic practices help in this matter.

Always share your wants, needs, and feelings with your partner. Sharing thoughts makes both of you understand each other better. Ask concretely and directly to your partner what you need and want from them.

Sharing your thoughts and speculations with your partner is always a good idea. You both should know what you both are going through. When you both think and reason each other, you both will be on the same page, and resolve issues will be more comfortable.

If you don't like anything about your partner, then it's best to tell him rather than bottling up the feelings. There are specific tips and exercises that will help to resolve the issue and problems.

If you want to discuss some issues or problems, then pick a neutral time to time. Timing plays a vital part in the relationships. Dull time means that when you both are calm and relax. A problematic conversation will only go well when you both are ready to deal with it.

State and tell the problem shortly and succinctly. Get on the point, and explain how it does affect you. Cut out the unnecessary details.

Avoid the blame game. The blaming and pointing out the mistakes of your partner will make him/her defensive and emotionally distant. It only will make things complicated.

Show Empathy more

Other than sharing your feelings and desires, it is essential to understand your partner. Try to see the situation and interpret it according to the perspective of your partner. Empathize with your partner. In order to do this, you have to put your thinking and perspective sideline.

To minimize the conflicts, you and your partner need to share the feelings often and take them supportively and constructively. This approach promotes the sense of safety even in the times of vulnerable and personal conversations.

Whenever you need to do a difficult discussion, you need to prepare yourself to forgive and open up to compassion. For constructive results, you must talk to your partner with a strong intent of understanding him or her.

Always try to be a safe haven for your partner. Partners need to feel safe with each other to make the relationship successful. This can only take place when you try to focus on one partner at a time. When one partner is explaining the problem, then others should listen and understand it.

When your partner sees that you are listening and understanding it, then he/she will be less defensive and will able to tell you everything that is bugging him/her. Listen without interrupting your partner.

Try to stay on the same topic while discussing a difficult question. It is easy to jump from one topic to another and from example to the example but don't do it. This will lead to issues, and your partner will not be able to answer them coherently. When the subject tends to shift continuously, then problems are not usually solved.

Respect is the vital element of every relationship. Always be respectful to your partner when both are going through heated discussions. Work on your anger issues. Being angry and exploding on your partner will erode your relationship. Seek therapy to cope up with your anger issues.

Be more forgiving

Every relationship faces hard times. There always comes a point when one of the partners ends up hurting the other. It can happen in anger or in out of ignorance. Sometimes misunderstanding also becomes the reason for fights.

Feeling hurt is excruciating and is very difficult for people who have attachment-related anxiety. They tend to think that they are unworthy of love and are flawed. They flood their minds with sad and depressing.

This leads to self-criticism and makes the relationship destructive. When the person is hurt, he/she tends to recollect the bitter memories. If you are related to this, then let go of the past and learn to forgive. By adopting the habit of forgiveness, you will be able to overcome the anger that is hurting your heart and soul.

How to know that is your relationship really worth it?

If you are confused whether your relationship is healthy or not then you need to look into some aspects. Whether your partner is emotionally available or not? Is he/she is responsive towards your needs and wants? Are the care and value both sided?

Support and care are essential elements of a relationship. Is your partner supportive in difficult times? Is he/she there when you feel sad and upset? Encouraging each other to pursue interests is also very important. Is your partner there to support and appreciate you?

This not only implies to your partner, but you should also be there for your partner as well. It is not essential to have a perfect balance, but being comfortable with the balance you have is vital. If you want your needs and desires to be fulfilled, then be expressive.

But if the circumstances are bitter and suffocating and you decide you leave, then formulate a plan that will help you to walk away. There is some recommendation that will help you in this matter.

Construct a support system. Breakups are painful, and you eventually need someone to lean on and share your profound and sad feelings. Share your honest opinions and struggles with close people, so they completely understand you and support you when you decide to end your relationship.

One of the most challenging parts while leaving a relationship is that you need someone else to rely on and support you other than your partner. You use to count on your partner to lean on and for emotional support, but now you need new people. Having a support system will help to comfort you and will provide you with a secure and safe base.

It's okay to feel unhappy and even cry when you feel like. When you lose an essential person in your life, it is natural to feel sad and lonely. Do not push your feeling under the rug. It is terrible for you and will affect your mental health. Mourn and give yourself time. Time heals everything. There will be a time if that person will no longer matter to you.

Keeping reminding yourself that you are a valuable person. Always remember your strength and power. This can seem challenging to do in times of misery and sadness. Consider and pay attention to what your friends and family like and appreciate about you. They interact and socialize with you because they want you and like you..

Choose right and healthy ways of coping with your stress and sadness. When you are going through a problematic hard time, it is always an excellent option to take care of yourself. Make yourself busy with your favorite activities. You might want to go shopping, eat your favorite food or have sex. Then go for it. If doing such activities makes you less stressful, then do them right away.

You have to be smart and considerate about them. You can make the situation worse by buying Porsche or eating a lot of unhealthy food. Take part in the activities that will make you happy in longer terms. Eat healthy and fresh. Walk and exercise daily. Sleep and wake up the appropriate time. Perform spiritual rituals to cope up with negative thoughts and energy.

Do some meaningful work. Doing meaningful work brings a sense of engagement, and that is a beautiful cure when you feel disconnected. Volunteering work at shelters and schools bring a feeling of comfort and peace. Gardening is also beneficial in such cases. Helping others brings a sense of having value and connection. You feel happy and relaxed when you help others.

You should be prepared to go back to your partner. There are probabilities that at some point in your life, you will think about the idea of going back to your partner. The good times will appear in your mind, and you will think about the mistake as well. You might also think about doing things differently and better this time.

Before picking his calls or meeting him again, think about the difficult time you've faced while living with him. Remind yourself why you left him. Talk to your supportive friend and discuss the situation. Finally, when you conclude that leaving him was the right decision, then remind yourself that this weak moment will pass.

Forgive yourself if you try to go back to your partner. There are times when you feel sad and lonely, then you try to reach your old partner. You will see yourself in the arms of your partner before you realize what you've done. When you realize your mistake, then put an end to it. Everyone goes through weak moments, so try to forgive yourself.

Ending note

Hopefully, this has provided you with the guiding light to reshape your relationship. By making minor changes in your habits, you can create a path towards a healthy and happy relationship. Compassion and understanding each other is key to a successful relationship.

Consult a professional

The information provided that might not be enough for you. Maybe you still not able to cut off the patterns of the anxious attachment. In this scenario, consider couples therapy. If you are the one showing the toxic behavior then go for individual therapy.

Develop a secure base with your therapist so that you can share everything. Your therapist will guide you and assist you to cut off the problematic behaviors and negative self-perceptions. Find a therapist with whom you can emotionally connect because there will be a lot of heartfelt discussions that can only be done with the person you feel connected and safe.

MICHELLE MILLER

CHAPTER 7:

Protecting Your Relationship from Affairs

Is your partnership descending? It is not easy to maintain a connection. Many couples face many bumps along the way to a healthy relationship. Until previously understood, these bumps may cause couples to step in the wrong direction leading to breakdowns or divorce. To avoid further harm, it is essential to understand many such relationship psychos beforehand. There are reasons why relationships fail, and when you know these causes in advance, you have a greater chance to save your troubled relationship. Although nobody can mention most the particular reason for the failure of relationships, we have listed the main reasons. So, what are these victims in relationships? Loss in contact or lack of coordination. One way to connect is to have good, regular communication between couples. Couples continue to fall away because of inadequate contact or loss of touch. Many issues with relationships begin with the lack of contact. Assuming you care what, your husband or wife feels that your partnership is dangerous. Misunderstandings and disagreements are often the product of your wife or girlfriend, not talking. If this occurs in your relationship, you will realize that this is one of the reasons that relationships fail and that you have to do something to improve communication. Not respectful of the aspirations, interests, and careers of each other. One of the reasons why marriages are collapsing is the difficulties between couples with jobs and aspirations. If two parties have conflicting interests and goals in a relationship and cannot agree or accept each other, the relationship will eventually fail. That is that two people have different goals and professions to seek, of course, so it is better to respect one another's desire or occupations to prevent pressure on the relationship in a relationship. It is safer for a husband or wife who trusts and respects the career of his or her wife or girlfriend to work with. Where it is not possible to achieve 100 percent appreciation, approval, and support, a friend or a girlfriend would at least be able to adapt and find a role with both their jobs and families. Sacrifices and sacrifices are inevitable. Obviously, they all will learn how to navigate their love-life careers. It's better to say than to do but not unlikely. There are couples who both excel in their careers while keeping a stable and healthy friendship.

Don't get along with friends and families of your girlfriend.

The friction with those nearest to the family or friend is one of the reasons why marriages collapse. Let's face it. You and your friend don't revolve around the world alone. You and your family can not exist without people like friends and relatives around you. Your friendship can not be compromised by not being close to your friend. If you and your partner's mother or best friend can't tolerate each other or live in a single room, the friendship can be difficult. Holiday meals and family gatherings will be unpleasant if the families and friends of your wife are not on good terms. It is best to get together with people important to your partner because you wish to build a healthy friendship with your partner. Things of life and luggage. Life baggage occurs, and complications as a relationship are formed may cause harm. A residual ex can spark envy, distrust, and resentment that will weaken your relationship today, so it's best to be sure that this is now in the past, and you are adamant about your relationship today. This is, therefore, inappropriate and damaging to equate your current relationship with your past relationships. Children and past marital complications can be daunting and can also influence your relationship, and you need to know how to handle with these issues to make the present relationship succeed. Another cause of relationship loss is the inability to manage issues and baggage in your life. Issues of capital. One explanation of why marriages collapse is financial problems. If not properly handled, money issues will ruin your relationship. Economic instability and hardship will eventually destroy a relationship. People or people who are overwhelmed by financial difficulties may become irritable, angry, violent, and cold towards their wives or friends, and they can eventually ruin a relationship. It is best to be frank about your financial situation from the outset, be open to discussing each other's investment patterns, money-sharing, and expenditures. With good and honest conversations, plans, and financial concessions, a tough couple can iron out problems and save their marriage.

Infidelity

Infidelity. It is difficult to sustain a relationship between two men, but involving a third person or abusing a girlfriend is a grenade that can ruin a relationship immediately. Infidelity is the greatest killer of marriages, and certain marriages cannot survive. Betraying your partner's trust is one of the key reasons why marriages collapse. There is no simple feeling to be replaced or cheated, which means that the cheated spouse or friend also leaves the relationship. Though there are people who can endure and make the relationship work again, it's best not to be infidel if you want a long-term partnership.

Disgusting behavior and behaviors.

While it is true that loving someone requires embracing all his or her flaws, there are also behaviors that can get irritating over time and may cause your partner one day to wake up and decide he or she needs to end the engagement. Only small issues like not putting the toothpaste cap on, not cleaning the bed, not putting the ground washing in the laundry, or getting the shoes and boots filthy in the house will be picked up because issues do not go well and your wife will break the relationship. Nagging, being a battle, arguing openly, insulting your wife or husband, calling or shouting disputes, hanging on to rancor, punching your spouse or partner when you're angry, tossing away too much or unfair anger, ignoring conversations about issues in your partnership, deception or dishonesty to your spouse or partner is a bad thing! Being in a relationship should help partners to be happier people and not get worse because it is easier to improve and create a good relationship than to have negative habits that will ruin the relationship in the end.

Things are a ritual in your relationship.

The fire and the desire in the relationship could die because you were too relaxed or content to have a routine rather than an act of love. You're looking more like family or friends than like lovers. Very relaxed with one another extracts suspense and passion from the relationship and makes it predictable and repetitive. When partners do the same thing over and again, as people and as friends, they stopped through. Shake your routine and spice you up. You can do different things and desires to evolve as an individual, and there are things that you can do to bind together. It is important to encourage your husband or companion to do his own thing or to enjoy the company of his or her mates, but it is also important to spend time alone with each other on frequent occasions or holidays in order to interact and build new enjoyable memories.

Intimacy and sex are absent.

Life can be too chaotic and difficult for partners to end up being too distracted or depressed for love or sex that is not appropriate in a relationship. Couples have to interact closely mentally and physically, and sex is the perfect way to do that. During a long-term relationship, sex will dry up, and partners appear to have fewer sex over the years. Couples are meant to discourage this. One of the causes why marriages fail is lack of affection or sexual dissatisfaction. When people avoid having sex, they appear to be isolated and withdrawn and are vulnerable to unfaithfulness. It is best for couples to lead a healthy sex life to keep the relationship alive and exciting. Although having your partner closely with you through daily sex is vital, couples should be aware of the pressure on your wife or girlfriend not to participate in frequent intercourse. There are studies that suggest that having daily intercourse once a week is acceptable and enough to sustain the romantic relationship between partners. There are many barriers to doing this, such as job pressures, pressures of your daily life, caring for children, and the situation in which you are not sexually mood yet, like all other problems in your relationship, the amount and scheduling of sex should be addressed and prepared. Intimate sexual connections are important in any marital interaction, and if partners do not have enough sex links, they have to do something to address this issue in order to save the relationship.

CHAPTER 8:

Rescue Broken Relationship

As time passes by, you and your partner might go through many difficult moments. The fact that you are still together proves that you both learned to navigate the difficult waters of commitment. But now, after so long, you feel you have fallen into a rut. You feel the relationship is pretty monotonous. It's not that you have unresolved issues, it's just that the routine has finally set in.

So, what can you do to preserve the flame of love alive? How can you help your partner be excited about the relationship again? Is there anything that you can learn to turn love back on?

Like the First Time

Do you still recall how the relationship used to be in the past? Do you have fond memories of when you began dating? Then use that to your favor. Treat your spouse the same way you treated him when you began dating. You may still remember how many details were involved in a date.

You were kind and loving with him. Why don't you attempt to talk to him with that same energy and excitement you had when you first got together? You liked showering with presents and letters. Why don't you bring back all of those special actions again? You liked hanging out together alone or even with friends. Why not try to do the same again?

Letters and presents help your partner realize that you still care about the relationship and him after so much time. Don't think that they are too cheesy! They might be just what your partner needs. You don't need to make them so elaborate. You only need to have him in mind.

Going out on a date in itself is an exciting idea. You can plan a date at the same place you had your first date. If that's not possible, you can think of a restaurant, park, or any other place that your partner might enjoy. Planning something together will also help you be united. Teaming with some friends will make it even more exciting and funny.

Don't limit your thoughts to just what you used to do. You can also try something new that you've been thinking about for a while. Even if it seems something that your partner might not like, why not inviting him to see if he's also interested in joining with you?

Affection Is Still Important

Stress is still an issue that many of us have to deal with on a daily basis. Affection can relieve that stress. Showing affection is still important as it was during the first days of the relationship.

Show consideration for your partner's good qualities. Notice how your partner displays his perseverance when going to work, his effort when helping in the home, his determination to commit to the relationship. His good qualities are what endeared him to you.

Strive to show how much you value his good qualities by telling him how you feel about them. Men also need to be told how valued they are in a relationship. You can have his good qualities in mind when congratulating him. The point is that you need to acknowledge these good qualities and be truly grateful for them. Be observant.

In the coming week, you can try to put effort into noticing what your partner does to add positively to the relationship. Even things that you may possibly take for granted. After much time, there's the risk of you taking your partner for granted or the other way around. You can easily start to focus, not on what he's doing, but on what he's not. Never underestimate how words of appreciation can have an effect on your partner. If you don't start feeling appreciation for your partner, it's easier for him to feel drawn to someone who does.

Take the Initiative

You should also be willing to take the first step towards keeping love alive. You may think that your partner also has to show some initiative since he's also part of the relationship. But your partner might be thinking the same!

Take the initiative by communicating how you really care about the relationship and your partner. Do nice things for him. Your partner might react in a very pleasant way. But even if at first, he may not seem to react in the way you expected, don't give up. It might take a little bit extra effort or consistency for him to see that you really want their love to turn back on.

One issue that refrains many people from taking the initiative is infidelity. If this has occurred to you, you know how difficult it is to regain trust. You may have felt his unfaithfulness was blown to the relationship. But there are ways you can take if you feel you want to give the relationship a second chance.

CHAPTER 9:

Some Example of Conversation and Dialogue in Different Day Moments

What does a relationship defined by good communication look like? Here are eight habits that couples who communicate well practice all the time. We'll give examples of the habits in action when relevant:

They express their appreciation for each other

Good communication is about staying in sync not only about hard things and conflicts, but also about positive feelings. Couples who communicate well are always showing their love and appreciation for each other. This can include thoughtful texts, little love notes, compliments, and nice gestures. Even on busy days when distractions abound, an emotionally-healthy couple always remembers to show each other some love, even if it seems small. This habit nurtures the security of the relationship, and both people never feel underappreciated or neglected.

Examples:

Text your partner "I love you" in the morning, so it's the first thing they see when they wake up.

Bring your partner flowers, their favorite snack, or a movie when you know they've had a bad day.

When your significant other does something around the house like cooking dinner, doing the dishes, or putting the kids to bed, say, "Thank you."

Send your partner a song that makes you think of them.

Tell your partner, "You look really good today."

Learn your partner's love language, and work on expressing your feelings towards them in a way they really connect with.

They make positivity a priority

Studies support the idea that intentionally working on positive thinking and reducing negative self-talk can actually make a person happier. The same applies to relationships. Couples, who actively make the effort to say positive things, especially during arguments, are happier and enjoy stronger relationships. A relationship with lots of negative energy is bound to make one or both of the people depressed, cynical, and frustrated. Instead of a source of happiness, the relationship becomes a source of stress. If the couple commits to being more positive, seeing the silver lining as much as possible, and expressing it out loud, both people get a boost and feel more secure.

They physically connect

Physical connection doesn't mean sex, though regular sex is often a sign of a healthy relationship. Besides that, other physical contact is a sign of good communication and can help improve communication. Whether it's hand-holding, back rubs, kissing, etc., physically connecting allows a couple to communicate without words. They get to know each other's nonverbal language on a deeper level.

Examples:

When you're watching a movie with your partner, sit with your legs touching.

Be physically close, like cuddling, without expecting sex.

When you're going for a walk, hold hands.

If your partner had a hard day and doesn't want to talk about it, offer to give them a back rub, foot rub, etc. instead.

When you're lying in bed relaxing, give your partner a head rub.

Always kiss and hug "Hello" and "Goodbye."

They listen to each other

We've talked a lot about active listening, especially in arguments, but listening outside of conflicts is a sign that a couple is communicating well. A couple who listens to each other will remember what their partner likes and doesn't like what they've asked them to do, and how they feel in certain situations. Neither feels like they always have to remind their partner about things, like chores or schedules. The same applies to body language; both people make an effort to notice nonverbal cues, so their partner doesn't feel that they always need to vocalize a feeling. They understand each other with a simple look or a touch, or at least pick up that their partner is trying to tell them something.

They validate each other's feelings

In a relationship built on empathy, the two people will make validation of the other's feelings a top priority. This means not getting defensive and making excuses for behavior or words they don't like. Instead, there's a lot of active listening, putting themselves in their partner's shoes, and respecting what they feel. Even if they don't completely understand where their partner is coming from or feel what they're feeling, they never dismiss those emotions. The mere fact that their partner is feeling something is enough. In healthy relationships with good communication, this validating is a two-way street.

Examples:

While your partner is talking, maintain eye contact and give encouraging sounds or words, like "Hmm mm," "I see," and "I get that."

Direct your body towards them, instead of away, and keep it open, so they feel like you are really there in the moment with them. If your partner likes physical touch, hold their hand or rub their shoulder while they're talking about something that makes them emotional.

Ask follow-up questions, so your partner knows you're still interested and committed to really understanding what they're saying.

If you notice your partner acting differently, take the time to ask them if something is wrong, and if they want to talk about it. This shows you are observant and not dismissing what you see.

If they seem insecure or embarrassed about their feelings, validate them by saying something like, "Of course you feel that way" or "I would feel the exact same way, too."

They aren't afraid to be honest and vulnerable

Honesty and vulnerability are essential in a healthy relationship. With couples who have good communication, opening up to each other isn't scary. The relationship is a place of safety, not judgment, so both people feel comfortable talking about anything and being themselves. The significance of being honest and vulnerable with one's identity can't be overstated. This gets to the root of good communication and the positive power it can have over a relationship. When communication includes empathy, validation, and no judgment, both people in the couple feel secure in them as well as in the actual relationship. This manifests as honesty and vulnerability.

They are flexible and willing to compromise

Seeing conflicts as puzzles to be solved together is huge for a relationship. When communication is good, both people are more flexible and willing to compromise. They aren't stuck on a specific resolution they believe is the best one; they're open to their partner's input and finding a solution that makes both people happy. Arguments are much less likely to get really heated and emotional when this is a priority.

They are able to take accountability for themselves

Couples who communicate well are not afraid to say two simple words: "I'm sorry." This phrase is short, but incredibly powerful. It's a manifestation of an ability to take responsibility for one's own actions and mistakes. It takes humility, which is a vital trait in any relationship. People able to recognize when they're wrong and apologize have let go of the need to always be in the right, or always "win." They can humble themselves before their partner and themselves. This type of "I'm sorry" isn't just skin-deep, either; it's a true apology that means the person is committing to being better in the future. A relationship between people willing to apologize and really mean it will last way longer and be much stronger than relationships where that isn't a practice.

Examples:

When your partner points out something that annoys them, say something like, "Oh, I didn't know you felt that way, I'm sorry."

If you say something during an argument that you regret, come back to your partner and apologize, saying something like, "I feel really bad about what I said earlier, and I want to say I'm sorry. Next time we're arguing, I'm going to try really hard not to let that happen again."

If you can, be specific about the mistake(s) you made, saying something like, "I wasn't being respectful of your feelings, and I'm sorry;" "I know you don't like it when I raise my voice, so I'm sorry for doing that;" and "I'm sorry I forgot to take out the trash this morning, I'll be sure to remember tomorrow."

CHAPTER 10:

Significant Habits of Good Relationships

Habits have a significant effect on your relationship. When it comes to having a good relationship, there are certain behaviors that can have a strong and positive impact. It's essential for you to be conciseness when forming routines, especially for your relationship.

Significant Habits of Good Relationships

You need to make an effort every single day to perform them, so they become part of the routine to you.

Always show respect

Showing respect for your partner is a habit worth making, as it is an ingredient necessary to create a happy, safe, and long-lasting relationship. You express your affection, appreciation, and comfort when you show respect for your partner. If you show contempt, you convey that your spouse is not acknowledged. Respecting your partner, despite variations, is all about valuing them for who they are. You may have a other view on life, but that doesn't mean you can neglect and put down your friend.

If experiencing conflicts, make sure you respect the disagreements between your spouses. This does not allow you to offend your partner in front of friends and family or in public. Also, show respect, especially when you're in disagreement. There will be moments when you disagree on a topic, and it's going to be how you approach this problem as a team that's going to make the world difference.

Go for a stroll with your friend

This is a ritual formed by a husband and where they find a deeper connection in their relationship. If you love nature and spend time with your mate, make it a habit to walk— either in the mornings before beginning your day, or at night. For example, husband and wife walk on Sunday mornings and in the evenings. It's a mental decision which they make to go out together every day. It encourages communication, fresh air access, and quality time. Once you develop this routine, the body may actually want to go out. It is noticed this with couples when they made it a habit to walk at night, and on Sunday mornings, their bodies became ready to spend the quality of time. Walking with your partner also promotes good fitness, and can be as easy as walking up and down the block. Decide how long and how often you'd like to walk with your partner; the major thing is to being on the same page and making sure you make the mental decision to build this routine together.

In the night time turn off the television and be with your friend

How can you relate to your partner when there's always television? There is no bond established when you both look at the television screen endlessly in the evenings. Take the mental decision to turn off the television at night, and spend time together in quality. You may be able to snuggle and watch a movie sometimes but avoid watching TV most evenings.

Take the time to chat with your friends about their day and how they're doing. The behavior causes love and attachment.

Snuggle up and chat on the sofa with your partner; talk to each other and what you two can do to strengthen your relationship. Whether it's preparing for the next holiday or your next date night, there'll always be something to consider. Focus on developing your relationship and discuss issues you need to tackle.

In the morning, take some tea with your friend. This simple gesture indicates a great deal to my husband. He loves drinking coffee and shows morning love and affection to get it to him. If your partner likes to drink tea in the morning, and through this act of service, create that habit, Express love. When you bring a cup of tea to him, it shows you care, and this is one way you can show love to him. Wake up a few minutes earlier so you can spend some quality time together with your partner before going on the job. This is an easy yet powerful habit of happy relationships.

Share positive attributes about your partner to others

'Habit of sharing positive attributes about your partner can help the relationship deepen. Alternatively, sharing negative attributes about your partner will only build a tall wall between you two. Would you know a couple who always argue with friends in public and show negative characteristics about each other? This is a bad habit that inevitably wrecks a friendship. This destructive behavioral pattern causes distrust, disconnection, and disrespect. Get used to projecting positive attributes for others. An optimistic behavioral trend produces respect, appreciation, and devotion.

Scroll down to read the article Are you reaching your full potential?

Take the life-potential evaluation of Life hack and get a personalized report based on your unique strengths, and find out how to start living your entire life and achieve your full potential.

Reconnect throughout the day

We have such busy routines that it can be the last priority to communicate with your partner throughout the day, but if you want a healthy, long-lasting relationship, reconnecting-connecting-connecting with your partner throughout the day is important. It is as easy as sending a romantic text or calling your partner on the way home during your lunch break. This habitude is meant to keep your partner linked and focused. You can still take the time to send a text message or send your friend a phone call, even if you have a hectic schedule. Render yourself artistic. Think about ways you can reconnect-connected-connect with your partner all day.

Take time to think

Take time to think out how you feel loved most and how your partner feels the most affection by looking at these 5 love languages. Imagine having a tank of love inside of you. Your love tank is filled up each time your partner speaks your love language. Your love tank runs low each time your partner doesn't convey your love language. When it comes to important behaviors of happy relationships, establishing the habit of speaking the love language of your partner on a daily basis creates in your relationship, passion, affection, and warmth.

Cooking and cleaning

The cooking with your partner is always much more fun. I know when John helps me; I enjoy cooking a lot more.

Cooking together builds intimacy, communication, and love; creating and eating food when you are with your partner becomes an intimate act. I express my love by cooking and eating with my husband (with TV off), which creates a deeper bond between us. This is a big opportunity to spend time together in quality.

If you prefer cooking or your partner, make it a habit that the other person cleans. John and I have a habit of cleaning up afterward whenever I cook, and vice versa. It shows appreciation for my cooking when John cleans after I cook and that he values me. It is important that you always love and respect your spouse, even if the cleaning of the dishes is as easy as that. It's nice to know John appreciates the love I put in my cooking, and it's a sign of love-affection to want to do the dishes Become mentally stronger!

Become Stronger

Every day shows love for your partner welcomes to your partner! It is just as simple as this. Whatever love you want to show in your relationship, do it. Do this on a single day. It's about showing your gratitude to your partner when it comes to important traditions of happy relationships. This can be leaving a love note at the end of the day before going to work or taking flowers home. It goes back to the love language of your mate. Find the language of love for your partner and show your gratitude for your partner through their language of love. If your partner feels valued by quality of time, make sure "turn off" and focus your attention on your partner when you get back home from work. Sit down on the couch, and be with your partner. Whichever language your partner loves, make sure you speak the same language. Make it a habit of showing your partner appreciation every single day.

Working together as a team towards objectives (short-and long-term)

A happy relationship focuses on short-and long-term objectives. Unhappy couples have nothing in their lives to look forward to. Focus on creating, establishing, and attaining goals within your relationship. Happy couples have ambitions, small as well as large. Follow this template setting target, and start cultivating your partner link.

Spend quality time

In the morning to show and be with a partner before beginning the day. Surely this practice starts to rob your relationship and the bond you have with your partner. We have such hectic schedules that it is even more important to take the time to talk with your partner in the mornings. Reflect and understand what brought you two together. It's easy to allow tension, anger, and distractions to get in the way of a happy relationship, but when you take the morning time to love and appreciate your partner, you're building a routine that's filled with comfort, affection, and care.

CHAPTER 11:

Cultivating New and Healthy Relationships

Allow Vulnerability

One of the first thing of being in love is when you become suddenly very vulnerable. This vulnerability is present in your feelings, longings, and fear. When you start to fall in love, your heart will open to your partner. You begin to entrust your heart to your partner and show yourself to them, as you do only with very close people.

You may be worried about being vulnerable, especially if you've had bad experiences in relationships. When you are open and vulnerable, those issues that were otherwise suppressed by you can come into your consciousness in new relationships. Therein lies the fear that is often justified - but don't allow it to scare you away. New relationships are just that - new. Judging them based on past experience isn't fair to you or them.

True Beauty Comes from Within

A different sure sign of falling in love is the capacity to see the inner beauty of a person. At the beginning of a romantic relationship, much attention is paid to the exterior.

Over time, as the feelings of love blossom, you will see the true personality of your counterpart - their true inner beauty. At this thought, the saying "love makes you blind" is confirmed.

The Family

If you are committed with someone who one day asks you if they can meet your family, you can be sure that the person is falling in love with you or even deeply in love with you. The family is very important and getting to know the family of your partner makes the seriousness of the relationship clear. If you have been introduced to both the family and the circle of friends, you can be sure that the feelings of your partner are genuine.

Selflessness

The last and clearest sign of falling in love is pure selflessness. This happens when you or your partner put the needs of both of you in the foreground and subordinate your own needs.

A one-sided relationship does not help you. Even if you feel that you cannot live without your partner and love them beyond measure, if both of you aren't on the same page, the relationship will go nowhere. Here are some ways to cultivate meaningful and healthy relationships in the early stages:

1. Be clear about what you need

On your first date, before your entrées have even touched the table, the both of you should examine what you truly want for from a relationship. Be clear about what you are looking for. In this way, you will both be on the same page from the get-go. The idea of this can be alarming, but in any case, learn to expect the unexpected. They just might disclose similar wishes.

2. Talk about your dreams and wants

Would you like to build a small home and live off the grid? Take a year off to travel the far reaches of the planet? Share these dreams with a potential partner. Discover whether your objectives compliment another person's and if you have overlapping interests. It's extreme more fun to find out about someone when discussing dreams rather than general hobbies.

3. Have wide open communication

If something is disturbing you, do not hold it inside because of a paranoid fear of what may occur if you bring it up. Address the issues and have quiet, caring discussions to see the two points of view. It's such a much-needed refresher to know you both want to cooperate to discuss anything before something turns into a major issue. It's not about being right or wrong — it's about the two individuals working together.

4. Accept each aspect of yourself

If you don't accept yourself for who you are, why should someone else? There may be aspects of yourself that you don't like or would change if you could, but they aren't important. The sooner you can look at yourself and be happy with everything you see, the better of you'll be in life and in love.

5. Manage stress together

Stress will never leave — it's the means with which we handle it that matters. When your partner is disturbed or stressed, be there for them to vent to. Don't attempt to fix it all; rather, allow them to work through the problem as they wish to. All they want is to know that you're there.

6. Offer thanks regularly

Having a mutual appreciation for each other is massively beneficial. It's also important to give thanks for other aspects of your life. Grateful people are happy people, and a couple that is grateful for each other is better able to build a healthy relationship.

7.   Talk about the big things

Talk about everything, from moving in together to building a home, from children to funds and family travels. Don't wait until these events are here - get a head start and begin discussing your expectations early. Many couples dread this sort of talk for fear that their partner will not agree with them. But the sooner you uncover differences, the sooner you can begin working to come to a compromise.

8.   Have dinner together

People bond over shared food, so make the most of it! Put on some romantic music, dress nicely, and connect. The meal almost doesn't matter as much as the full, undivided attention of the both of you.

9.   Be available

When you need your partner, do you want them to be available, or will you be able to deal with them prioritizing something else over you? If you wish to be put first, start by putting them first. Be ready to come to their aid if they need you. You don't have to drop everything on a whim, but ensure you know what you're going to do if they ever let you know that they're going through a crisis and could use your support. Your actions in their time of need set the tone for the future.

10.   Work toward being a better partner

If you're like most people, there are things you wish to change about yourself. Some of these desired changes can positively affect your relationship. By striving to be the best person you can be for the one you love, you're also becoming better for yourself.

A solid relationship is two people cooperating to build a life together. A solid relationship is somewhat similar to a trinity, two people make something more profound and superior to themselves, yet they are still themselves. For a relationship to develop, you should likewise develop as an individual and not lose yourself.

Enjoy Being in Love

Are you newly in love? Then you are probably feeling great right now! I have a few good tips for you to help you get the most out of your love and keep it strong for a long time.

Additionally, talks should not be neglected despite the romance. Celebrate your shared romance, because it gives strength for less good times and creates a great common ground. Conversations are just as important as experiences, though. Share your feelings with your partner and give them the opportunity to get to know you as well.

Tips for a Long and Happy Relationship

The following tips will help keep your relationship healthy for a long time.

Avoid nagging

Any kind of criticism of your partner's idiosyncrasies either leads to quarrels or makes you feel annoyed. Psychologists are of the opinion that criticizing your partner in many cases is a projection of your own shortcomings.

Rather than frustrating your partner with complaints, you might think about what makes you uncomfortable about their traits, and work on reframing your viewpoint.

Understand that your partner is their own personality

You must accept the fact that your partner is an individual with a unique personality. Nevertheless, we subconsciously and sometimes consciously treat our partner as if they are an extension of ourselves. Accept that your partner is a being with a character of their own with appropriate feelings and perceptions, opinions, and experiences.

Accept your partner's mistakes

To err is human. Your partner is not an angel, so they are bound to make mistakes. When that happens, learn to forgive and do not capitalize on the mistakes of your partner.

Above all, there are lots of things we cannot change about our partner, so rather than grumbling or nagging, why not learn to live with them? Small mistakes are not a matter of life and death. If you find it difficult to cope with your partner's idiosyncrasies, call their attention to it, and explain yourself in a polite manner. Don't blame or accuse, simply discuss.

Do Not Tolerate Destructive Behavior

Learn to tolerate your partner as long as their behavior is not destructive or life threatening. If you discover that your spouse or partner is very aggressive, don't paint over the situation and learn to "cope." Your safety is important. If you ever feel threatened, don't stick around to try to keep the peace. Get out.

Take Emotional Time Out

Our skin needs sunlight for the production of vitamin D. However, prolonged and frequent sunbathing can cause life-threatening skin cancer.

So, the right dosage is important. This applies to relationships, as well.

Of course, we need each other to fill our lives with happiness. But we also need emotional time-outs in which one does not think of the other person or is involved in the planning of joint activities.

Meet alone with friends or join a club alone to develop yourself as a person. If both partners experience something different from each other, there is also something to talk about at the dinner table.

Be Faithful and Sincere

Unless you have made other arrangements, share a duvet exclusively with your romantic partner and no one else. To be deceived and cheated on by a close person is one of the cruelest experiences that can happen to anyone.

If you really love your partner, you will spare them that experience. Ultimately, faithfulness builds such deep trust that you can't replace or fix it once broken.

Address Problems

No partnership is in complete harmony. You are two different personalities with thoughts and feelings. A relationship, no matter how much love and dedication you feel for each other, is always the result of many compromises.

Therefore, face critical matters head on rather than waiting for the other to address the problem. Couples therapists unanimously agree that communication is the key to a long, healthy, and fulfilling relationship.

Appreciate What You See in Your Partner

The first infatuation does not disappear forever, most of the time it gives way only to another feeling, that of deep attachment and love.

You have found that you can rely on your partner, that they think of you, and in so many ways suit you perfectly. That you as a couple harmonize and like to be with one another.

CHAPTER 12:

How Do We Work Together

It might seem impossible to work together at this specific point in time, but you can start answering this question by remembering when you last worked together.

Look at the timeline you made and recall the ways you worked together to resolve problems. That should tell you what you should do now.

The ways you worked together need not be deep. For instance, it could be as simple as the time you two worked on a garden together. It could be the way you each do your part for Thanksgiving every year.

It will you figure out how you can work together on some of the specific problems in your relationship.

When you worked together for Thanksgiving, who did what? What problems did you run into while you did this task together, and how did it turn out? What did you two do to make things work out the way they did, for better or for worse?

From here, expand to more everyday ways you already work together without even thinking about it as working together. That includes chores, financial planning, and the like. As you found out in the "How do we relate to each other?" question, we don't always work together in ways that we acknowledge in marriage, because all the things we do together are so intertwined into our daily lives that it just feels normal. But the more you reflect, the more in touch you will be with how you are already working together.

The problem is, when we are working with our partner on more challenging tasks, we are more aware of the fact that we have to work together. If we aren't aware of that, we will make a lot of mistakes.

We like to think that in a previous life, we've been very good at showing our partner how to do something even though in this one, we have to do a lot of things in a row that we aren't very good at. Sometimes we know what we are doing, but other times we don't. It is the problems that we do not see coming that make it harder to work together in a productive way.

We want our significant other to admit to their crimes — and part of starting again is admitting fault and apologizing. We may want to think that we couldn't have done anything wrong. As we've been trying to be more aware of throughout, though, none of us are perfect, neither you nor your spouse.

You won't abruptly become more perfect because you are pretending to be. All you are doing is being dishonest with yourself in a way that is extremely counterproductive to working through your issues together. You are better off being yourself in all of your flaws, so you can both at least be open about your flaws and work with them.

Now that you have thought of a time that you two worked together for Thanksgiving and times you work together every day; the next exercise will be about practicing working together right now.

It may be an exceedingly simple task, but it will test how well the two of you can work together so you can (1) get the task done and (2) do it without bickering too much.

Together, find a new meal that you can eat tomorrow. The catch is that it does have to be new, so you can't just say you'll make one of the dishes you cook all the time and be done with it. You need to find a new recipe in a cookbook or somewhere else and then make a plan to get all the ingredients, determine who will do what, and come to an agreement about all of this.

As an extra challenge, I want the two of you to try to get this done in just fifteen minutes. Start a timer as soon as you can, and then get started. When you are done, come back to the workbook so you can have a discussion.

Read on only after you have already done the exercise. Then, ask yourselves some quick questions. What went wrong? What went right?

You should also ask yourselves if you met the two requirements, which were to get the task done and to do it amicably.

Start off by each telling the other what you did right. You want this to be a positive exchange before a negative one. They want to hear good things from you first, and that's a principle that you should apply throughout these exercises: whenever possible, try to let the positive come before the negative.

Only after you cover the positive should you move on to what could improve. Take note of how I didn't say what went wrong, but what could improve. This way, even the negative things sound more positive. It may not seem like it would make a big difference, but it really does, because negative and positive attitudes are contagious.

When you and your spouse learn that you can each work through your disputes without it being filled with negative emotions, you will stop dreading it so much, and you'll get excited to work through things together because you'll know that it doesn't have to be so bad.

It might sound like this couldn't possibly be the case right now, but if you give the methods outlined in this workbook a real shot, you'll see that they really work. It's just that you need to be able to imagine how things could be different.

Sometimes, we lose sight of why we even try to work with our spouse. We may even have thoughts like it isn't worth the pain to work with someone else.

But remember that everything in life comes with benefits and drawbacks. It might sound like it would be better to be alone, and it might seem like everything would be easier. Of course, in some respects, everything would be easier just for not having to work with someone else anymore. But there is more to it than that.

When we have the opportunity to have a spouse who will be there for times that would be difficult alone, we shouldn't take that for granted.

No one can deny that sharing and working with other people can be harder than doing things on our own sometimes. When we get frustrated working through the same problems every day with our spouse, we can't help but think that we would be able to handle it better alone.

Try this. We have issues that we don't think are serious, but affect every aspect of our relationship. What do we think is important to us in our relationship? What do we believe is critical in creating a strong marriage?

But how can we achieve this understanding of what really matters to each of us? By taking the same observations that we used, to begin with. The same questions that we asked before. To turn on the kind of self-talk that will improve our relationship, we must see ourselves through the eyes of our spouse.

But the truth is, you don't even appreciate all the things that are having someone there for you helps with, not the least of which being sheer emotional support. On the surface, it may seem like a small thing, but having someone there for you feels much different from when you are going through hard life experiences such as job loss, the passing of someone we love, and so on all by ourselves.

We don't even think to appreciate having our spouse there when these things happen, because, by their very nature, these things are still so rough to go through.

But try to remember that it would be harder without them there. Try to remember that the most important thing they do for you is just being there. Do all you can to be there for them, too?

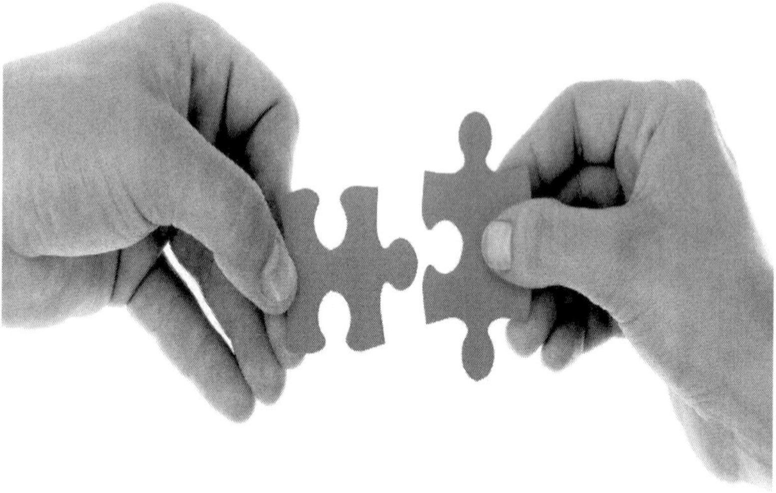

CHAPTER 13:

Practice Empathy

The heart of a romantic relationship is empathy, according to Carin Goldstein, a licensed marriage and family therapist. It is the heart of all human relationships, but we have a bias towards romantic relationships.

It is through empathy that we can understand and maintain the relationships that we build. Compassion, or in the words of the Dalai Lama, Emotional Awareness, is our ability to recognize the emotion not only within ourselves but also in other people. When you are empathetic, you may get to experience emotional resonance. Emotional resonance is when you encounter another person's emotions as your own, to the extent that you feel their pain and pleasure.

When you and your partner get comfortable around each other after dating for a long time, you will find that, with time, familiarity sets in. So, you begin not to take their emotions as seriously as you did at the start of the relationship. Familiarity breeds contempt, they say. When you stay with someone for so long, you tend to become accustomed to their presence. So, you no longer put effort into understanding them. Because of this, you then grow distant from your partner. You do not put effort into communicating with them, and as such, intimacy suffers, you break the trust, love becomes an illusion. All this is the result of a lack of empathy. And it is what breaks a lot of relationships.

According to psychologists, we will often experience different types of empathy;

Affective Empathy. This type of empathy involves us understanding the other person's feelings and then responding appropriately.

Somatic Empathy. Somatic empathy is the kind of compassion that is more pervasive. When someone experiences somatic empathy, the individual gets to feel, physically, the distress the other person is going through. If the other person feels pain, you also feel pain.

Cognitive empathy. This kind of understanding involves you understanding the other person's state of mind and what is going through their mind when they act the way they do. You can put yourself into their minds and understand what would make them make the choice they do. You may not agree with how they react, but you put yourself in their shoes for a better perspective.

To be a better empath, you need to have a great understanding of all three and know how to experience them with regards to the situation.

So, how do you build empathy in your relationship?

How to Build Empathy for a Happy Relationship

Become More Self Aware

As with any other situation that relates to how we can improve our relationships, self-awareness is the top priority. When you are open with yourself about your emotions and feelings, you will then become more in tune with who you are as a person and how you deal with these emotions. When you come to terms with how you deal with your feelings and work to improve them, you will then begin to feel the emotional resonances of others around you.

So, to become more empathetic, begin by going deep within yourself. This understanding of who you are helps you become intimate with who you are and then work on how you build intimacy and trust with others.

Be Vulnerable

We are all scared of being vulnerable. Have you ever gotten into a relationship, but because you are afraid of the other person hurting you, you hold back. Since you view the other person as being capable of destroying you, you also become cold and callous. These are defensive measures we often take when we do not want to be vulnerable. When you put a wall around yourself so that you are not sensitive, what happens is that you also do not consider other people's feelings. In this case, you become cold and distant to your partner, thus breaking down communication between the two of you.

But when you begin to make yourself open up about yourself emotionally deliberately, you will find that you also become more receptive to other people's emotions. In this case, when you take the time to open yourself up to your partner, you give clear indications that you trust them. In return, they will also share their feelings with you intimately, bringing the two of you closer. Even if they do not reciprocate and hurt you, you come to understand that it has nothing to do with you but with them. So, you let go, knowing that you are doing your best to become a more emotionally intelligent person.

Listen to Understand

Active listening is one marker of empathy and emotional intelligence. It is what brings you closer to others and helps you build a rapport with others.

When you listen, you gain a deeper understanding of what other people are going through. You learn about their emotional state of being. What they feel and how they feel about things becomes your issue too. You do not need to agree with what they are saying, but you understand where they are coming from. Active listening is how you develop emotional resonance, which is what leads to a growth of intimacy with your partner.

When you are empathetic, you do not center your feelings if your partner is talking about their passion. Here, you sit back and listen. You try to understand them, and they, in turn, will make the same effort to follow you.

Consider Your Partner's Emotional Truth

Sometimes, your partner might not express how they feel directly to you. But to be empathetic is to be emotionally intelligent. You should contact their emotional resonances, either through reading their body language or their tonal variations and choice of words. Then, show that you understand them by expressing the feeling that they are having a hard time communicating. 'I take this to mean that you are angry/saddened/hurt by what I've said.' When they affirm, do not be defensive. Apologize and make a point of taking into consideration their desire for you to change.

When you do this consistently, you will find it become easier to feel your partner's pain. Empathy takes time, but when you make deliberate efforts to building it, you will improve the dynamics of your relationship.

Ways in Which Empathy Improves Your Relationship

You Humanize Your Partner

When you practice empathy deliberately, you take note of your partner's humanity. When you stay with someone for long, you tend to overlook their humanity. Dehumanizing the other person is why many relationships crumble; because the couple forgets about each other's humanity.

But when you begin to practice empathy, you never let go of the knowledge that your partner is a person that deserves your compassion and understanding. This way, you communicate better with them, you listen to them better and learn from them too. You also provide them with love and intimacy, which we all need.

You Learn to Regulate Your Emotions

When you develop empathy, the first thing you learn is self-awareness. Self-awareness then allows you to create the understanding that your emotions are not more important than other people's feelings. Have you ever come across a person who feels as though their opinions are more important than others? It's annoying.

When you become more empathetic, you begin to learn how to limit your emotions and take note of your partner's feelings. You learn to deal better with your emotions without feeling overwhelmed, and in turn, help your partner deal with theirs.

Better Conflict Resolution

Building empathy is building a connection. When you and your partner are more empathetic to each other, you bear each other's emotions. Thus, when you disagree, you will often go through the conflict with a desire to see out the disagreement without letting your emotions get the better of you.

Rather than blame each other for the different views, emotional intelligence, the basis of empathy, allows you to look at the situation, not your partner, as the problem. Rather than direct your dissatisfaction at your partner, you direct it to the issue.

Improved Intimacy

Your partners' feelings become your feelings and vice versa. Empathy develops an understanding of your feelings as well as those of your partner. You develop affective empathy. You relate intimately to how they feel. This affective empathy then grows into somatic empathy and then cognitive empathy. This empathetic intimacy allows you to grow beyond just being in love. You become each other's place of refuge. This closeness improves your intimacy and will enable you to grow closer still.

Empathy is what will determine whether you and your partner will get along when you follow any other related advice. It is empathy that will allow you to listen to your partner actively. It is empathy that will make you trust them, and they, you. This understanding then guides you to make the right choices to manage a crisis.

CHAPTER 14:

Couples and Compromise

The basis of a good relationship depends upon your skill in being able to compromise. Two people can be deeply, intensely, passionately in love and yet not be able to live together. For living together demands the capacity and will to compromise—not just once, or now and then, but continuously in a thousand little ways, all day long.

At night in bed, do you want one blanket, two blankets, or none? Is this a good time for sex or not?

If it is time to eat, are you both hungry? Do you want to eat the same thing? What movie do you want to see? On and on, when you live with another person, both trivial and major life events demand continual compromise.

If all is going well, the process of adjusting is so easy it almost goes unnoticed. On the contrary, if it is not going well, every moment, every trivial issue has the potential to become a major conflict.

The Meaning of Compromise

Compromise can mean different things to different people.

What is compromise?

Perhaps you think compromise means having to give in. Or, on the contrary, perhaps you think it means your partner should have to give in.

Not so.

Compromise is a process whereby each of you gives a little, in turn, until a mutually satisfactory agreement is reached. For each act of giving, something must be given in return. It is like balancing a seesaw.

The further apart you are, the more difficult it will be to reach a compromise. For example, you may have little difficulty resolving which movie you want to see, but it is a decision of another magnitude to decide where you want to live, or whether or not you want to have children. In some cases, keeping the relationship may demand major sacrifices for both partners.

Sometimes Compromise Can Bring Rewards of Its Own

Mary and Tom had come to see me because of conflicts over money, but then, during one of the sessions, issues came up in regard to their vacations. Tom was a surfer who loved the ocean. He really didn't like the desert at all. Mary, on the other hand, loved the desert but couldn't care less about the ocean. This difference caused constant bickering. Neither wanted to go on a vacation separately; after all, the fun of vacationing was really the pleasure of being together.

What to do?

"Why not compromise," I asked. "One time try the desert; the next time, the ocean?"

They were reluctant—particularly Tom, who said, "I hate the desert; too hot!" Nevertheless, they agreed to compromise. Tom would try to put up with the desert if Mary would accompany him to Hawaii and watch him surf.

Following the end of their sessions, I didn't see them for several months, until I happened to run into Mary in the grocery store.

Guess what?

They had followed through on the compromise. They had gone to Palm Springs for the desert vacation, and Tom had had a wonderful time at the music festival. And Mary had loved Hawaii, even though she didn't want to go in the water, just sit on the beach and watch Tom surf. Compromise had not only improved their relationship but had enriched their lives.

And then there is the story of Francis and Scott, whose compromises were more difficult to make but that made a big difference in their relationship.

Frances and Scott had been married about ten years. They had had a good marriage, but bickering between them had increased to a point where they were feeling chronically angry with each other.

Frances was somewhat overweight—twenty pounds—and Scott would make an occasional comment such as, "I see the cookies disappeared," or, "I thought we were going to skip dessert." Comments Frances didn't respond to but that stayed with her and were upsetting. Yes, she had eaten the cookies, and yes, she had meant to skip dessert, but no, she didn't need to be reminded of this.

And then Scott, who had been a fairly heavy drinker for years, had increased his cocktails from two martinis before dinner to three. Frances would say each time, "Do you really need that third drink?" and he would say nothing but would go ahead and have the drink anyway. Then they both would feel irritated.

When these interactions and the bad feelings associated with them came out in the session, both Frances and Scott wanted to change them. They agreed to try to reach a compromise. Francis would talk to her physician about her weight and begin exercising, and Scott would save the third drink for special occasions.

An important part of their agreement was that they would be responsible only for their part of the compromise—they would not criticize each other for failing to carry out their part. They would be as supportive as possible.

This was not easy for either one of them. Despite good intentions over the next few months, they each had relapses. Frances still occasionally ate cookies or dessert when she shouldn't have, and Scott still occasionally had that third drink when he shouldn't have. However, Frances had seen her doctor and begun exercising, and Scott had taken seriously her request to keep the cocktails at two rather than three. They were quite supportive of each other, praising each other when they were successful and remaining quiet when they were not. When I saw them a year later, Frances had lost ten pounds, and Scott had (for the most part) kept the cocktails at two.

Frances and Scott were lucky. Although compromise is always worth a try, certain problems, such as weight and addictions, are difficult to handle on one's own and can require outside help.

Sometimes a compromise is asking too much. If you feel you cannot go that far, you have to say to your partner, "I'm sorry, I can't do that. You are asking more than I can give."

For example, if one of you lives in Alaska and the other in Florida, and neither one of you is willing to move, your differences are too great. A compromise is not possible, and you will have to say to each other, "We love each other, but we cannot live together."

Sometimes one partner will make immense sacrifices to adjust to the other, but this may well lead to grief. A compromise needs to be mutually satisfactory, otherwise the decision rankles beneath the surface until it finally comes to a head.

Staying with another for years while swallowing one's own wishes may be an unwise decision. Painful as it may be, it is far better to be open and honest as to one's feelings. Putting the cards on the table, where they can be talked about and worked with, is far better than the seemingly easier "going along with it" and having the hope things will eventually change on their own.

CHAPTER 15:

Know Your Partner

The more you know and are willing to learn about your partner, the closer you will become and at a much faster pace. Finding a few bits of information to identify with will help offer you reassurance that you've found your forever mate. You don't want to be identical twins about everything, but a few things in common gives you an instant bond. Some areas such as goals and values are important to be on the same page for relationship success.

Know the History of Your Partner

Knowing a few of the basics in the history of your partner and openly sharing your history will give each of you a foundation to begin exploring more in-depth. You can't be expected to remember everything in the beginning but build on information as time goes by. A few of the things to start with could be:

- Where they were born.
- Where they grew up.
- The size of their family.
- Where their family is located.
- Education level.
- Profession and job experiences.
- Any past serious relationships/marriages.

- Any children and where they are located.

A small amount of information to start will allow you to initiate conversations that lead you to learn even more. It's important to have enough information to feel comfortable that you are making a great choice in partners.

Discuss Life Ambitions and Goals

What are your goals in life? Are you wanting to live in a big city or have dreams of a small cottage near the woods? Do you like fancy cars, or is an old 4X4 pickup all you'll ever want and need? What are your ambitions with career, home ownership, salary, retirement plans, and savings? You can find out the same information in return. It's vital to ensure you and your partner have ambitions and goals that line up with one another or you will end up a miserable person.

Know their Core Values and whether they Line up with Your Own

Core values are the value you place on things like honesty, integrity, work ethic, compassion, and more. It would be difficult to establish a long-term relationship with someone that did a little shoplifting or found lying to be no big deal if those are not your values as well. It's a recipe for immediate disaster. Most core values are established before the age of six, although it doesn't mean that values can't be added to and expanded over the course of your life. It's good to know where you're starting at and see where things align and where there are potential problems.

What are their Tastes in Music, Movies, Books, Food?

Great conversations require a good supply of basic interests and knowing what their tastes are in music, movies, books, food, fashion, and all things current or trendy. The better you share the intricate likes and dislikes of basics in life, the wider the arena is for powerful conversations. It's also nice to know areas you may differ, at least slightly. It can help expose you to something different you might end up loving just as much. Every person that loves Mexican food never realized it until giving it a try. Sharing new experiences forces you to look at your favorites in a new light. It can breathe new life into what had become stagnant.

What is their Favorite Color, Animal, Car, and More?

Keep it going! You aren't finished in the learning process if you are going to become a true expert in your partner. You still need to discover important things like what is their favorite color, favorite car, favorite animal, and whether they prefer gold or silver. It's almost as if a floodgate opens and the conversations become powerful and filled with vital information. It also provides plenty of clues on what you can get for birthdays, holidays, and anniversaries. The sky is the limit in asking the question but try and spread out the questioning over a long period of time.

Are they a Deep Thinker or Impulsive by Nature?

How a person communicates can have a lot to do with their baseline personality. You'll be able to make observations as easily as they can see where you sit on the spectrum. More reserved, deep-thinking individuals often seem to have fewer words to say. They tend to place a lot of emphasis on the words used, however. It could be that they are introverted. It doesn't mean they are shy but more deliberate and selective in action.

A more impulsive person is generally considered an extrovert. Although it may appear to be all over the map, the tasks and conversations are skillful and done in their own special way.

You'll find that the more impulsive personalities hardly ever run out of conversational topics. Most are upbeat and highly energetic. Making these simple observations can point you in the best directions for starting and continuing a conversation.

What are some of their Basic Habits?

Learning a few of their basic habits will help make you an expert on your partner. Do they go jogging every Monday and Wednesday morning? Is there a show they have to watch on Friday evenings? Do they prefer to drink coffee out on the patio on their day off? Do they have an irritating twitch to their eye if you leave a dirty dish in the sin after a midnight snack? Studying and understanding the habits of your partner will help you work more in unison and help create a happy home environment

What do they need from a Relationship?

All parts of information you gather culminate in showing you what they are looking for and need from a relationship. Ask the important questions, assimilate the information, and use it to help create a smoother transition into the relationship. (See figure 5)

Figure 5 – The process of discovery and learning about your partner.

Learning about your partner should be something you look forward to on a daily basis. Most successful relationships are not based on a perfect fit. It's finding ways to fit together in the uneven areas that make the difference. Finding ways to grow together is the ultimate goal.

CHAPTER 16:

Couples Therapy Exercises for Improving Communication

Viable communication is the lifeblood of any relationship. For some couples, merely figuring out how to convey emotions, resolve conflicts, and offer with one another is a challenging endeavor. Utilizing a couple of basic couple's therapy practices for communication can do miracles to support you and your accomplice manage issues and develop nearer. Learning communication skills that can allow you to appreciate the marriage or relationship you have wanted continuously is significant. By setting up a superior discourse with your accomplice and figuring out how to share your sentiments and address issues with less conflict, it will be conceivable to make a relationship that is healthier, stronger, and all the more emotionally satisfying.

Using Positive Language

Couples therapy activities can extend your emotional bond and allow you to manage muddled circumstances and issues without lashing out or contending. Utilizing positive language when you speak with your accomplice might be the absolute best approach to make an increasingly successful emotional discourse. It is all too easy to wind up baffled, especially if your relationship has hit an unpleasant time. Bending over backward to embrace a positive and empowering tone during your discussions can turn what might have generally turned into a warmed contention into an open door for positive development and progress. Being excessively basic or receiving a negative tone might cost you numerous chances to sustain and strong. This activity, when polished after some time, can allow you and your accomplice to develop nearer.

Communication Exercises to Build a Lasting Relationship

Learning and applying couples therapy practices for communication can do a lot to reinforce your relationship. Managing touchy issues and sensitive issues can be a strenuous endeavor. Tools and activities that will allow you and your accomplice to more readily share and convey what needs be can demonstrate to be an essential piece of making a healthier and all the more satisfying relationship. Poor communication might do unmistakably something other than restricting your capacity to manage common issues. Activities that have been intended to make communication quality as opposed to risk can help guarantee a more drawn out and more joyful relationship. Figuring out how to improve as an audience and rehearsing the skills that will allow you and your accomplice to develop nearer makes it feasible for you to appreciate another degree of understanding and gratefulness for one another.

Active Listening

Numerous couple's therapy activities are based around rehearsing skills that will improve you and your accomplice audience members. Undivided attention is intended not just to make it easier to banter about touchy issues but also actually to develop your understanding and valuation for your accomplice. When rehearsing undivided attention, it is significant for the speaker to stay focused on a single idea or point. For the audience, focusing on sharing their accomplice's point of view while endeavoring to find new bits of knowledge about how the person thinks and feels can be of incredible advantage. Regardless of what subject is being examined, the most significant piece of undivided attention is to do it with persistence and love. Tending to how your accomplice feels as opposed to merely responding to what your accomplice says is essential for successful communication.

Learning to Grow Closer

Individuals change and develop after some time, regularly in manners that are amazing or startling. Being in a long haul relationship can make it easy to ignore new features and aspects of your accomplice's character. Couples who think that it's challenging to acknowledge who their accomplice has developed into will likely experience difficulty imparting. Couples therapy works out, for example, learning undivided attention skills and sharing emotions uninhibitedly, can enable you to build up a superior feeling of who your accomplice is. Indeed, even the most agreeable endeavors could be bound to disappointment if you can't understand and identify with how your accomplice's advantages and passions may have changed after some time.

Sharing Emotions Freely

Numerous couple's therapy practices for communication are intended to diminish conflict and make a progressively successful path for you and your accomplice to share what you are feeling. When it is challenging to examine emotions without starting a contention or causing a battle, working through issues and differences may also be unimaginable. Talking about what you need to have a sense of security when sharing how you both feel can be useful. For some, couples, having a specific time or spot to examine significant issues or to take a shot at the structure, better communication may have any kind of effect. Set aside the effort to ask your accomplice what might make that person feel progressively useful when sharing your emotions. At that point, put these ideas energetically to help guarantee that your future endeavors to improve your relationship are as successful as conceivable.

Taking a Trip Together

Keeping up relationships requires a great deal of diligent work, which is the reason it is significant for you and your accomplice to unwind and loosen up. Masterminding an outing with your accomplice can give chances to you to take a shot at structure excellent communication while having some good times. Following a similar everyday practice or remaining in a safe environment can eventually cause a relationship to stagnate. Sharing time together in another condition will allow you and your accomplice to make new recollections while alleviating the pressure that could be making communication unquestionably progressively tricky. It's also regular for couples to go on couples withdraws where the very purpose of your outing is to improve your relationship.

I Feel

Expressing your sentiments in a manner that is easy to understand can be a precarious endeavor. Starting your announcements with "I feel" can give couples a progressively powerful approach to organize their considerations while offering the audience data that is easier to grasp. This is one of the numerous couple's therapy practices that can be used to handle sensitive issues that can prompt contentions. By isolating the manner in which you feel from the original conditions and occasions being examined, you can support your accomplice feel not so much guarded but rather more ready to tune in.

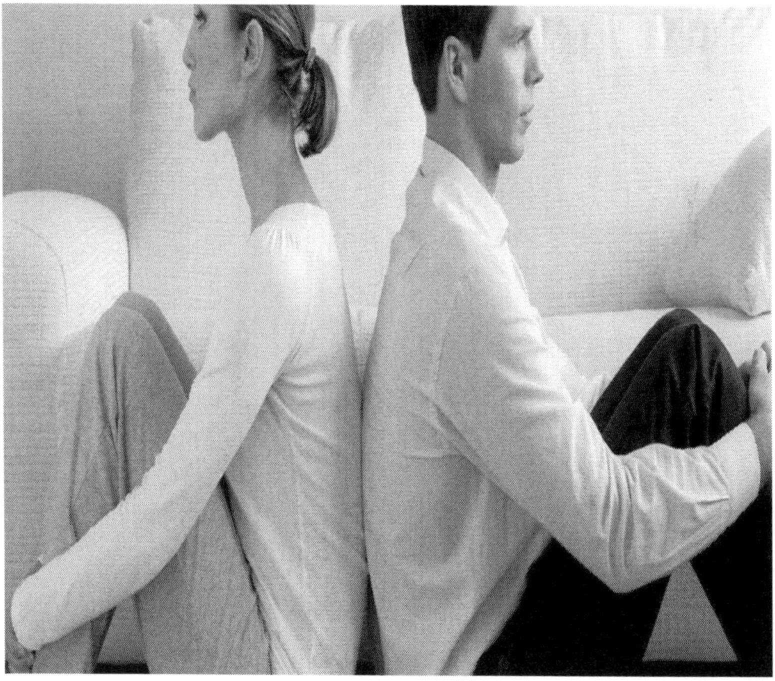

CHAPTER 17:

Steps to Set Relationship Goals

About Setting Relationship Goals

Did you know that the laws of motion can be applied to your relationship? Yes, I am not joking, and it is true! The first law of motion states that an object will not move until an external force is applied. The second law states that an object will accelerate only when an external force is applied. The third law of motion states that every action has an equal and opposite reaction. These are three simple laws and can be easily applied to any relationship. By applying the first law of motion, you will realize that your relationship will continue to exist the way it is and will not change unless you make any changes. This applies to things both good as well as bad. For instance, if you are tired of the way you both deal with arguments, then this pattern will not change unless you both make a conscious effort to make the change. According to the second law of motion, you cannot make any changes unless you make a conscious decision to do so and put in the necessary effort. The third law of motion is perhaps the most easily explainable one. The way you act influences the way your partner reacts. Now, the same concepts can be used for setting goals in your relationship as well. When you set goals, it gives your relationship the required momentum to keep going. When you and your partner come up with certain mutually agreeable goals to improve your relationship, you can create an assignment that is conducive to your relationship's growth. The goals you set will help avoid your relationship getting stagnant. Setting goals is quite easy, and the chances of success in attaining these goals increase when you set simple goals. The relationship goals you come up with will help you and your partner concentrate on your relationship even when you hit a rough patch. Once you come up with goals, you must make sure that you are both willing to put in the necessary effort to attain them. Establish goals yourself and allow your partner to do the same. You can sit down together, brainstorm, and come up with relationship goals for your relationship together.

Make it a point to set goals about communication, love, compromise, commitment, sexual intimacy, household chores, and support. These are the main aspects that influence the quality and strength of your relationship. Once you cover these areas and come up with attainable goals, you can improve and strengthen your relationship.

It is quintessential that you and your partner both work on improving the way you communicate with each other. While setting goals in this area, think about ways in which you can improve your communication.

I am certain you love your partner, but how expressive are you? If you don't express your love, how will your partner ever know? How often do you express your thoughts? I'm not suggesting that you need to keep telling your partner over and over again that you love them, but there are little things you can do which convey your love for them. For instance, sharing in on any household responsibilities, cooking their favorite meal, or giving them a hug as soon as you wake up in the morning are all ways in which you can show your love for them. In a long-term relationship, it is quintessential that you express your love and affection for your partner.

A relationship will not last if there are no compromises. My way or the highway kind of thinking can quickly shatter any relationship. Instead, learn to compromise. It is okay if you don't always get your way, and it is okay if you are not always right. Start making an effort to understand your partner's perspective. Learn to negotiate and understand the importance of coming to compromises. When you compromise, it doesn't mean that you are wrong while your partner is right, it merely means that you love your partner more and are willing to concentrate on the relationship instead of any other petty issues or problems.

Emotional intimacy is as important as physical intimacy in a relationship. So, make a conscious effort and set certain goals for physical intimacy in your relationship. Be a responsive and caring lover to your partner. Spend some time and discuss with your partner about all the various things you want to try and be open with them. Learn to cater to not just your needs, but the needs of your partner as well.

A common problem a lot of couples run into is related to household responsibilities. I believe in the equality of partners, and therefore partners must share all responsibilities. After all, you are living together, so why not share the responsibilities? Spend some time and come up with a schedule to divide responsibilities between the two of you so that one partner doesn't always feel burdened with household work. This is quintessential, especially if you and your partner have day jobs to attend to as well.

Tips To Keep In Mind

Happiness doesn't always come from getting what you want, but it can come from moving toward what you desire. When it comes to relationships, it essentially means that couples must have a couple of goals they are moving toward together. So, how can couples support and motivate each other to achieve their individual goals along with the relationship goals? Well, here are some simple steps you can follow to ensure that you and your partner reach your goals while maintaining the health of your relationship.

The first step is to ensure that your individual goals are in perfect alignment with your relationship goals. This alignment is quintessential to create a sense of harmony, which allows you both to attain your personal goals. Once this harmony is present, there is no limit to the things you can both achieve together as a team.

It is time to make two plans - a six-month plan and a two-year plan. Think of this as short and long-term goals for your relationship. Have a discussion about what you plan on doing, where you want to be, and how you want to be within these two timeframes. The next step is to visualize and think about where you want your life to be in the next five, 10, 15, and 20 years. Ensure that you both maintain a positive attitude, and don't casually write off any ideas until you have both had a chance to express yourself first. Don't judge your partner, and don't allow your partner to judge you. Keep an open mind toward each other and attentively listen to what the other person has to say.

Spend some time and make a list of all your personal goals. You and your partner must do this individually and then spend some time together to discuss the lists you both made. You can take all the time you need, and carefully note down everything you wish to attain in life. Include short-term as well as long-term goals and discuss this if you feel like you're getting stuck while making this list.

Whenever you are setting any goals, the goals must be such that they make you feel good about yourself. If the goal you are setting for yourself or for your relationship goes against everything you believe in, you will not be able to achieve it. The goals you set for yourself must not only be good for you but must be good for your relationship as well. When you have shared goals, it not only becomes easier to achieve them, but the health of your relationship also improves along the way.

Regardless of the goal you set, make sure that the goals are specific, realistic, and attainable. If a goal doesn't fulfill even one of these conditions, then you are merely setting yourself up for failure. People often think that setting lofty goals for themselves is a good idea. They seem to stand by the age-old adage of, "If you shoot for the stars, you will land on the moon." Well, I don't think this is the right way to go about setting goals. After all, if you don't attain your goals, it will be a source of massive disappointment and discontent. To avoid this, ensure that the goals you are setting are realistic, attainable, and quite specific. You and your partner must come up with an arrangement that helps you stay focused and accountable for any commitments you make to each other. The relationship you share with your partner is quite sacred, and you must cherish and nourish it. The arrangements you create must support you and your partner along with your relationship. It's not about getting rewards or punishments to create accountability. It is about coming up with a mutually beneficial plan to create accountability to each other.

It is okay to concentrate on your goals, but it is not okay to overlook any victories you attain along the way. Attaining your goals is seldom a sprint and is always a marathon. So, the journey to your goals matters as much as the goal itself. You and your partner must be appreciative of each other and each other's accomplishments. Rejoice in all the small wins that happen in your lives. Celebrate each other's successes. By doing this, you are naturally cementing the bond you share. If you celebrate every milestone you cross, it will give you the motivation to keep going.

You must be supportive and understanding. Support and encourage your partner to achieve their goals, and your partner will reciprocate these gestures towards you. Give your partner the room they need to attain their goals and don't become a hurdle. Keep a conscious check on any criticism you dole out. If your partner is making a mistake, feel free to correct them, but do so gently.

Be each other's support system. There will be days when you or your partner simply don't have the motivation to keep going. In such instances, be each other's cheerleaders. Your relationship will be happier and more satisfactory when you know you have your partner's support, and the same applies to your partner too. In fact, make it a point to seek feedback from your partner to see how they are doing. By asking for their feedback, you are not only making them feel important but are also giving yourself a chance to view things from a fresh perspective. Spend some time and make a note of all your goals. Keep reviewing these goals as you go about your daily life. Your goals can change, or the way you want to achieve them might change. You might also need to tweak your goals occasionally. So, don't forget to include a weekly review session of your goals. The final step is quite simple - always remember you are a team. Achieving goals becomes easier when you are doing it together. You don't have to do everything by yourself, and you can count on your partner for additional help or support.

Once you have accomplished your dreams or goals, don't forget to come up with new goals. Goals give you the motivation to keep going!

CHAPTER 18:

The Importance of Having Fun to Couples

A strong, healthy, happy, and long-lasting relationship does not just happen. It is a conscious effort by both parties, where each partner sees to the betterment of the relationship and each other in all ramifications. Dull, droll, lazy, boring, and annoying are definitely what you'd want your relationship to be described as. Fun-filled, interesting, happy, and joyful are better words you would want your relationship to be described with. It is understandable that things change in a relationship, and things move from how they were at the very beginning where you both met to become more mundane. With increased meetings, house chores, jobs, children, and other impromptu activities that spring up here and there in a relationship, it is only important that couples find a way to balance every part of their lives. The importance of being spontaneous and playful in your relationship cannot be overemphasized. It takes away the burden of having to constantly sit down and speak you mind and painstakingly explain certain things to your partner because when having downtime, there is a bond that is fostered. Your partner knows you more and can figure out your boundaries. Having fun with each other in a relationship helps increase your affection for each other. Imagine saying something and having the other person laugh so hard and then noticing that they have a particular trait about them you never noticed. The relationship is strengthened when you are reminded that the source of the other person's laughter and joy is you. The implication of this is that the possibility of you both getting a divorce anytime soon is very low if at all existent. Couples who have fun are happy and tend to spread this happiness around even beyond their relationship. It rubs off on the kids, in the church, at the office, and even amongst the people in the neighborhood. While it might be easy to fake that you have it all rosy at home, or that you dread going home every time it is mentioned, having to pretend is not healthy.

In a relationship, there is nothing more important than being united. Your ability to stand for your partner, come what may, is often as a result of coming to know them through constantly interacting and having fun with them. Having fun with your partner breeds unity; you learn to forgive quickly, you learn to overlook certain acts of the other person even before they apologize. It does not mean you should allow your partner to take you for granted or be manipulative. Ensure that being playful with your partner does not rob you both of communication and the other necessary factors for a healthy relationship. If your partner is one who constantly gets you angry without seeing the need to apologize (or if their apology never sounds like they are sorry), then you might want to sit and work that out before allowing it to slide and perhaps breed more negativity in your relationship. Don't allow constant fun between yourself and your partner take the place of real apology in your relationship when your partner has done something wrong. An apology is appropriate, and it could be done playfully so long as they mean their apology, and you do not feel shortchanged in your relationship. Another benefit of being playful with your partner is that it breeds hope. Hope for better things to come in the future. It is not unusual to see people in marriages as if they cannot wait for it to end (even after saying 'till death do us part'). It should not be that way. Many times, the reason for this feeling is that couples have lost hope in the marriage - they feel they are merely passengers in the marriage instead of the drivers of their marriage who take charge. What hope does for you is that it assures you of the future even when you do not know what that future holds for you two. Having fun with your partner reassures you and keeps you optimistic about the relationship. There's just that joy when you rough and tumble, and laugh with your partner that assures you everything will be alright between you guys. This is what hope is all about; you are positive in fun times with your partner that the future will be better and that whatever hurdles are present can be overcome. Being playful in your marriage rubs off on your children as they grow and your children are the best legacy you can leave the world with. No one wants to have annoying, angry, and sad children around them. Statistics have shown that nurturing kids in a happy environment tends to boost their positive outlook and helps them strive for better things in life. Children who grow up in a happy and playful environment tend to be more optimistic, and they approach failure as a stepping stone rather than a setback. Your playfulness as a couple also rubs off on your family at times. There are stories of marriages that have survived the hostility of family members (perhaps because the couples are from different countries or religions and the family members did not support the marriage) simply by being constantly happy in their marriage.

What then does it mean for couples to enjoy some recreation time in their relationship? Having fun with your partner could be described as a pleasurable manner of having fun at a discretionary time. Of course, our definitions of what is pleasurable in a relationship may differ. But, taking from the analogy of cake, fun time with your partner is the icing which should not be sacrificed. Research has shown that having fun and bonding in a relationship is not only a pleasurable activity but also a form of developmental activity. Just like the way children, while growing, learn a lot from interacting with their peers and playing games and having conversations, we also learn a lot about our partner from playing with them. It was Plato, a Greek philosopher, who said that what could you learn about a person in one hour of laughing and having fun with them, might not be even be understood about that person in one year of conversation. So, in having fun with your partner, you learn a lot about them and yourself. For example, how your partner reacts to losing a game played with you might just be the way they would react when they are let go from a job or lose someone dear to them. The manner your partner behaves during certain moments might just be indicative of what they would do in the real world. It will show if they are the type that takes responsibility for their actions, if they laugh at and look down on others who have experienced failure with pride, or if they treat people like they are part of the same team. Recreation time with a partner reveals to you a lot about your partner, and this knowledge can be garnered covertly, as opposed to typical dialogues.

Some persons see recreation time as childish. There is a video on the internet of a groom who had slapped the bride on their wedding day, simply because she had tried to be playfully mischievous with their wedding cake as she attempted to feed him. The point is, playful activities in relationships are not taboo. We should not be ashamed of them. You probably shouldn't say things like this to your partner: "lower your voice and stop laughing like a kid, the neighbors will hear us." While every relationship does not function in the same way, how about loosening up a bit? Nothing positive, good, or healthy comes out of a relationship unless the partners have consciously worked towards making it happen. An interesting fact here is that many people, before agreeing to be in a relationship with someone, may not mind the fun and games. There is a possibility that this all changes upon entering a relationship. By this time, it becomes immature to laugh in a certain way or behave in a playful manner. It's quite funny when people see or interpret playfulness in relationships as an act of childishness. The advantages of being happy in a relationship are not debatable, and neither are the advantages of being playful. It's important to state here that being playful in a relationship does not guarantee everything that has been explained above in the form of advantages, but the possibilities of these advantages coming forth are quite high. Here are some tips you should consider to spice up your relationship.

Schedule time for fun

Most couples intend to have fun but never really get around their business schedule or household chores or dealing with kids to really have fun. Fix a time for recreation on the calendar. If some time is allotted for you both to have fun, then you would get around having done so one way or the other.

Spontaneity

You should not make having fun bureaucratic or mandatory. Make your relationship as spontaneous as is reasonable considering what both of you are used to and can adjust to. Having fun should not be a do or die affair, it should be something that you do because you want to enjoy each other's company and not because the calendar says so. It's important that you find time for downtime at some point in your relationship. The reason why a calendar is important is for situations when you have been so busy for too long that (though you are not quarreling or drifting apart from your partner) you no longer have time to throw funny jabs at each other.

Variety

Having fun should be pleasurable and could and should include playing games, going to the movies together, having sex, looking at old pictures together, etc., so long as it involves something pleasurable that keeps you both happy and promotes intimacy. To help you and your partner spend more time having fun, it is important you learn healthy habits and try to exude positive energy all the time.

Loosen Up

Give yourself the opportunity to be a kid once in a while in your relationship. Be open to new things, and don't let your relationship make you lose your wonder. Look forward to new things and be ever ready to learn, especially when it has to do with new and untried ways of having fun with your partner. Be willing to speak to your partner about anything. Communicate your fears and concerns about things to them. This is wisdom about communication that can be learned from little kids. Most times, we get so caught up in being perfect adults that we forget how to be kids or begin to see being playful as being childish. It's not childish to tickle your partner out of the blue when tickling them makes them laugh. Learn to confide in your partner. It's easier to find the voice to tell your partner uncomfortable things when you both are out having a good old playtime.

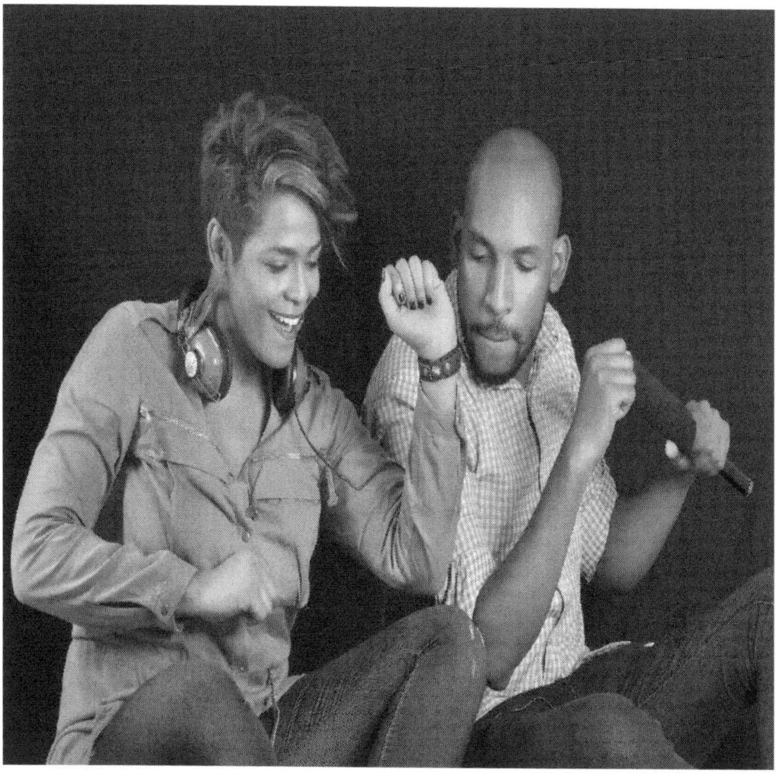

CHAPTER 19:

Learn How to Apologize

One critical way to build trust, rekindle intimacy, and connect emotionally with your partner is to learn to apologize when you hurt them. In the long-life journey of love as a couple, there will be moments of arguments and broken promises, which will result in hurting each other's feelings. At such times, learning to say "sorry" can save your relationship. Learning to apologize to your partner is a crucial life and marriage skill. It is difficult to say sorry or apologizes to your partner, especially if you belong to the class of individuals who view that as a sign of weakness.

Sometimes, neither of the partners is willing to apologize or admit their mistakes when they are wrong. This is a sign of pride and selfishness and only serves to make the situation worse. Let's say that you have had a heated argument or fight with your partner. Such an argument tends to make you feel awful. You find yourselves caught up in power struggle and a lousy tradition of waiting for the other person to admit their faults first creeps into your marriage.

You should learn to take the initiative, admit, and accept your faults, especially when you know you have made a mistake or when you are wrong. Sometimes, you don't even have to be wrong to apologize. As you will learn with time, it is usually not a matter of being wrong or right in the marriage, but just a difference of opinion. At such times when you feel that both of you are wrong, and you are wondering whether you should apologize to your partner, just do it! This is not a sign of weakness but a path that helps you become a better spouse.

When you understand what it means to you and your spouse, offering an apology becomes easier. Apologizing is one way to show that you are selfless, and you care for your partner's feelings. It shows that you are treating your partner the way you wish to be treated when you are hurt. It is a simple way to admit your faults, and that you are willing to correct yourself and try to do better next time. It is a way to own up your mistakes by acknowledging that you are an imperfect human being, and you can be wrong sometimes. It shows that you are willing to make an effort to grow from your mistakes and become a better partner.

When you make an apology, you learn to strike a balance between your pride and struggle for power in your relationship. By learning to put your ego aside and embracing selflessness, you can become one with your spouse and grow together, appreciating each other's mistakes and weaknesses. You can save your marriage or relationship by learning to apologize. But how do you learn to say that you are sorry and mean it? Let us look at some of the ways through which you can master the art of saying sorry so that you can save yourself and your spouse a lot of marriage or relationship woes.

Admit your mistakes

The first essential step in learning to apologize to your husband or wife is to admit that you a human being, and you are eligible for making a mistake. This makes it easier for you to accept that you have a problem, and you are wrong in one way or another. Unless you accept that you are wrong, your apology cannot be genuine, sincere, or meaningful. You will just say it for the sake of avoiding a further argument, and it may not reflect your actual position, attitude, or facial expression. So the first thing is learning to admit and accept your mistakes. Show that you are willing to be fully responsible for what you did and take the necessary corrective measures going forward.

Learn to respect the emotions of your partner

When our partners do something wrong, we get hurt. Anyone who has been in a relationship knows this to be true, and it is a rule with no exceptions. All of us feel hurt when it happens. As you approach your partner for an apology, after doing something wrong, it is good to keep this in mind. Show that it wasn't intentional and put yourself into your partner's shoes. This will show that you respect how they are feeling, and you will do your best to avoid making them feel the same next time.

Be sincere with your apology.

Listen to your partner as they vent out, and do not interfere until they have finished explaining how they feel. This will help you understand their perspective and the extent to which your actions have hurt them. That way, you will be able to offer a sincere and honest apology that reflects your true feelings and attitude towards how they feel. Don't begin to give explanations as to why you did what you did or start to give excuses. This will be a sign that you don't care, because you will be trying to justify your deeds. Be as specific as possible in your apology and just focus on that one issue at hand, which your partner has raised. Don't go outside the topic and bring a mix of other past problems into the picture. The bottom line is that you should never say you are sorry for the sake of pleasing your partner. You should be sincere and honest by being specific with your apology. This enables your partner to know how sorry you are, and will help you strengthen your intimacy, rebuild trust, and enhance how you communicate as a couple.

Humble yourself and ask for forgiveness

It shows how humble and caring you are to your spouse when you present yourself in person and offer a face-to-face apology. You may want to write a letter, send an email, or a text message, but that should come as a way to emphasize what you have already verbalized. If you find it hard to face your spouse and verbalize the apology, then you need to dig deep and unearth what is preventing you from doing the same. Don't be that kind of a spouse who gathers the courage to communicate face to face only when they are fighting. Master the courage to face your partner and offer an apology. After making an apology, take it one step further and ask your spouse to forgive you.

Forgive yourself

To show compassion to your partner, you must be able to be compassionate with yourself first. To be able to welcome and accept your partner's forgiveness, you must be ready to forgive yourself too. It may not be easy to forgive yourself, especially after realizing the severity, or the extent of the emotional damage you have caused your partner. Forgiving yourself gives you the confidence to work on yourself and make critical changes that will help you rise above your mistakes. Failure to forgive yourself can make you begin to play the victim. You may end up with inward resentment, which can make it hard for you to forgive or accept forgiveness from your spouse. This can limit your chances of becoming better.

Create an action plan

You don't want to keep on apologizing all the time for doing the same things. The best way to avoid the same issues from cropping up all the time is to come up with an action plan. You need to come up with a list of things or steps you will follow to avoid repeating mistakes. It makes no sense to your partner when you keep on repeating mistakes and apologizing every time you do so. If it was a communication mishap, focus on improving your communication skills. If it was delayed payment of some bills, come up with a way to remind yourself of such responsibilities. You can set a reminder on your phone or the calendar.

In other words, tell your partner the measures you are going to put in place to prevent the same from happening. Don't do this alone, but seek the feedback or the input of your partner while devising your action plan. This shows that you value their views and opinion, and they can see the effort you intend to make to turn things around and change for better.

Put your action plan into practice

Take bold steps to practice your action plan. There is no amount of rhetoric which can take the place of what you do. As they say, action speaks louder than words. Let your actions from that point on, reflect your commitment into making sure that the same issues don't arise again by acting your words. Change your behavior by putting the requisite effort to make up for your faults. This will eliminate any fears or doubts your spouse might have developed as a result of your mistakes. They will begin to rebuild their trust and intimacy once they see that you are putting a lot of effort into becoming better.

CHAPTER 20:

Accepting and Sharing Opinions

Some people, when they start dating, think that having differences in opinions about politics, religion, values, or morality means they will always be fighting over things from day one. This is far from reality and only becomes a problem when both parties refuse to take into account each other's viewpoints. Instead of accepting them or viewing them as a new perspective, they perceive it as something negative and thus, are always trying to change them. Opinions can be changed, but they don't always have to. If we take things back to the day you two met, was it not your differences that attracted you to each other in the first place? There is a strong backing behind opposites attract – proven both by science and psychological experts.

Having a different opinion does indeed complicate things slightly in a relationship but there are many ways to deal with it.

In this, not only shall be looking at these, but we shall also learn about why people have different opinions, why they should be accepted and appreciated.

I Have Something to Tell You?

The moment couples start living together, they are bound to come across diverse opinions – most of which may not match yours. This can lead to misunderstandings as well as arguments over even the smallest of issues such as what to dress your kid as on Christmas. If you come from a Jewish family and your partner is a hardcore Christian, this argument may seem quite valid as Christmas isn't a celebrated holiday according to the Jewish tradition. They celebrate Hanukkah instead. The same differences can also be seen in how the money is spent in the house, who gets to make the final call, who gets to discipline the kids, who is responsible for housekeeping and raising the kids, etc.

But where do these differences come from?

For starters, we all come from different households, neighborhoods or different sides of the country. Partners may have been raised in a certain way that conflicts with the other's way of living. In some houses, it is considered bad to talk back to your husband; whereas, in some homes, nearly all the major decisions are taken mutually after thorough discussions. This diversification of environments and early childhood experiences play a crucial role in personality development. Your partner may come from a family that spent every summer vacation out in the woods, but you may have never experienced anything as outdoorsy. Therefore, when it comes to taking the kids to someplace, your partner may insist on renting an RV and heading for the woods while you might be more interested in visiting the entertainment hub of the country for some family time together.

Then, we also have different educations, different exposures, different jobs, and different perspectives about life. All of these can easily become problematic when going unheard or unresolved.

However, these differences don't mean that your partner is right and you aren't or in any way demean you. Accepting others' opinions is a crucial aspect of every marriage. A relationship can be fostered with unity and understanding where every different idea gets discussed with an open mind.

Why You Should Listen to What Your Partner Has to Say

We believe everyone should see the world as we do. We think of it as the right way and are rarely keen on changing our minds about it. When we are paired in a relationship with a partner who has a completely different point of view than yours, it is so easy to blame them for being misinformed or living with a distorted opinion about reality.

But they think the same about your views too. So how to go on living with them when you constantly feel that they are wrong and vice versa?

First off, each individual is entitled to their opinions. Opinions are formed based on real events and make the individual who they are.

They aren't wrong, just different.

When you two are journeying together, keep in mind that it is never going to be easy or simple as a straight line. You both chose to be together and thus must provide each other with some space and understanding about the things they solely believe in. Having a partner with a different opinion is also a healthy thing for many reasons. For starters, it will enrich and broaden your vision about reality. Next, it allows you to question your own beliefs and opinions and see if you are wrong. A different opinion can also give you the chance to ask them what made them think that way or why do they believe what they believe in. The newfound information can help you two understand each other better and strengthen your relationship, as then you will be more considerate when discussing important issues with them.

Thirdly, when you acknowledge and accept your partner's opinions, they will feel more valued and understood. When they feel that, they will be more open with you and feel safe sharing their deepest thoughts and ideas with you without feeling judged. The level of trust between you two will blossom, and your partner won't need to amplify their views just to be heard.

It also helps to bridge the gap between you two as you learn to respect each other's viewpoints. Moreover, there may be times when one of your decisions may require more thinking on your part and your partner may help you see it. For instance, you are thinking to get a new job. You are thinking of a good pay raise and fewer working hours. However, you might overlook aspects like long commute hours and heavy traffic. If your partner knows how frustrated you get when you drive for long hours, they may ask you to reconsider. You might feel a little taken aback by their idea and believe that they don't want to see you succeed. But when you two sit down to discuss why you think it's a great idea and why they think otherwise, a different point of view may change your mind. You may come to realize that their worry wasn't about you earning more but rather about your mood and health. So a different point of view can help you see past all the glittery stuff.

You can also visualize the long-term impacts of your decisions. For instance, if we follow-up with the same example as above, your primary objective was short-term goals. You just wanted to work a few hours less and get paid more. However, your partner's concern was more about your health. Who knows, ten days into the new job and you are back to hating your life again and regretting ever leaving your previous job.

A difference of opinion can also help you overcome your weaknesses. As humans, we have the habit of underestimating our skills and talents. We always think that we aren't good enough. That is your opinion of yourself. Chances are, you may have backed down on some good potential opportunities in the past due to the same fear. Now enter a partner into this situation who thinks no one can beat you at the skill you are good at. This positive and refreshing boost of an entirely different opinion of yourself will improve your self-confidence.

How to Resolve Contradictory Opinions without Fighting?

Differing opinions will arise between partners – that's a given! How you are going to resolve them is the more important question. Sometimes, these differences in views can become the reason for fights and arguments between couples. So how can they move past that and accept and respect each other's opinions without breaking into a fight?

We have some great advice to offer. Take a look!

Negotiation

Negotiation or compromise is a suitable way to come out of a difference in opinions during complex situations. When you two want to do something your way and the partner intervenes with their methodologies, opt to compromise. Find a way in which neither one of you feels left out or disrespected. If you two can't reach a consensus and aren't; willing to give up on your stance, it is best to avoid attempting it at all. After all, nothing can be more important than your relationship, right? Don't be hell-bent on proving yourself right all the time.

Don't Argue

Sometimes, it can be very hard to change someone's perspective about things because they are very personal to them. In that case, it is unfair on your part to expect them to give it up. You must understand where they are coming from and why they think a certain way. If no mutual ground can be found, you must retreat.

Be Sensible

What your partner is saying might be rational, and you know it, but if you continue to argue, then that is just egoistic on your part. Try placing yourself in your partner's shoes and look at the world from their eyes for once. If you know that they are right and you keep fighting for the sake of being right, then you need to back up and accept it as a mature individual.

Don't Force It

It is unhealthy to impose your beliefs on someone and expect them to abide by them fully. No one ever said that differences of opinions are a bad thing. Forcing someone to think a certain way because you think it is right isn't justifiable. That would be acting childish. Express your mind and let the other person decide if they think it is right or not. Don't force it upon them.

Act Mature

Could they be right? Hey, we all can be wrong at times. At least, accepting it will let your partner feel valued and also leave you with some newfound knowledge. You are totally not too old to learn something new.

CHAPTER 21:

How Couples Therapy Helps

Couples therapy is intended to explain the personality discrepancies between people in a relationship to more efficiently solve problems. Couple therapy is a fast, solution-centric approach that describes and takes the outcomes into account clear and achievable recovery objectives. Couples therapy allows couples to develop relationship enhancement approaches.

The pair therapy approaches teach you how to take constructive chances in establishing a romantic relationship. Opportunities for personal development persist throughout the lifespan. Individual development contributes to healthy, engaged ties. Couple therapy encourages relational development that allows people to feel more connected. People gain trust when they feel confident to expose to their partners the darkest, most private self. The best way of obtaining a successful outcome is to partner with an accomplished specialist including a licensed marriage counselor and a family therapist.

Which kinds of issues are dealt with in the consultation of couples?

Psychotherapy for couples deals with common issues in relationships, including inadequate communication, difficulties getting along, and boundary conflicts with other family members such as parents or grandparents, parental disputes or financial stress. Couple counseling teaches couples a more caring and compassionate way of living.

Employment or job, financial and child and family problems are the pressures that modern society imposes on a relationship. Through marriage therapy, people learn how to cope with daily challenges without damaging their relationship. Through psychotherapy, couples understand that we are all imperfect and that we all have human flaws. Couples in counseling gain an awareness that we are both capable of harming one another and learning strategies to avoid it as much as possible. Partners in the therapy process feel that they have a safe place to identify negative behavior. People learn good communication skills in relationships to apologize for and to express sorrow.

How long do people live in pairs?

Counseling for couples is structured to deal with unique issues. In 10 to 12 sessions, problems should be detected on average and effective behavioral approaches start to take effect. The number of sessions is adjusted according to the couple involved and their specific problems.

Many couples want to work with the therapist to develop new skills and successful approaches. They know that cognitive instruments that lead to a more productive partnership can be taught. When a few put into practice what is learned during the original sessions, they are inspired to "learn more," because they see that they have a happy life with their partner. Couples frequently initiate marital counseling in a situation of crisis. If heavy emotions begin to withdraw, the psychotherapist and the couple will begin the real learning work and develop other skills and strategies to strengthen marriage or relationship.

Why do you use a marriage and family therapist (MFT) for counselling and psychotherapy for couples?

Marriage and family care practitioners, who have a certificate in marriages, family dynamics and psychotherapy, are specially trained. These experts diagnose and treat a broad variety of emotional and psychological problems among people in a relationship.

A marital therapist is professionally trained to listen and unbiasedly examine the problems posed by partners. The couple's friends and family are always caring and want to help, but their deep emotional involvement in one or both partners leaves them unable to consider the dynamics of the relationship critically. Just after the first session with a successful marriage therapist, it is very normal for couples to have "hope" in their relationship that they do something good.

Can I become a better listener by offering advice to couples?

During couples' therapy, people learn different methods of responding to the needs of their spouse. Effective listening strategies enable people to build their partner's empathy, helping them to understand better and strengthen their relationship with their partner. Relationships and relationships are improved and cherished when people learn to listen to each other.

Psychotherapy for couples includes instruction in dispute management, the removal of miscommunication and painfully hurt emotions. Any unavoidable partnership causes issues. You should listen entirely to your partner's needs through counseling. An accomplished marriage therapist, a family and couples may help people to develop their communication skills in a special way.

The therapist will help you keep track of a question while working on it. You learn to avoid "making a case" by carrying insignificances that can only cause suffering to others. Couple counseling can help establish dialogue surrounding a difference of opinion that leads everyone to a suitable solution.

Why is counseling couples going to help me overcome my marital conflicts?

Next, for both parties, the therapist should help develop a secure, warm and trustworthy relationship. So you meet with the therapist to grasp the conflict's existence. Conflicts also occur when partners vary in intent or expectation in a relationship. The therapist helps you and your partner to consider each other's needs and to learn new ways of interacting to overcome the conflict.

An experienced couple therapist may help couples to build communication skills to strengthen dispute resolution techniques that can be developed over time. People develop an improved willingness to listen to the views of the other person, although they may not agree to the specific question. In a non-critical and non-confrontational manner, the marriage therapist will demonstrate successful and reliable ways of communicating negative emotions like hurt and rage. Efficient resolution of disputes leads to couples becoming stronger and more secure, strengthening their marriage.

Is therapy for couples really effective?

Many studies indicate the importance of therapy for couples. The vast majority of people in pair counseling show a change in their understanding and relationship.

Couple therapy does not only allow people to remain together very effectively. Nevertheless, as each person in the relationship continues to grow and evolve, they progress to more efficient, constructive contact and successful conflict resolution outcomes outside their relationships in their lives. Person therapy is not a passive "done" for a person, but a "service" with the psycho-therapist. The counselor and the couple have positive communion in order to achieve positive outcomes.

Couple counseling is an efficient way of recognizing the relationship's actions of spouses and allows an effective resolution of relationship problems. A couple counselor deals with a number of different problems and helps couples learn to work together more lovingly. Couple counseling varies in length to provide ample room for different issues in connection. Professional marriage and family therapists are highly qualified professionals who can promote impartial and comprehensive care for a couple. Those attending marriage therapy learn some skills for better listening and dispute resolution. Overall, people find that couples therapy is successful and that their well-being and relationships are strengthened overall.

CHAPTER 22:

Things You Should Do Before Marriage

You have reached a place where you know who is the one you want to spend the rest of your life with. You popped the question and now you are preparing for the big day. However, there are a few things you should consider doing before starting officially your lives together. Let us take a better look at what are those things.

Before getting married, you should clarify which are the career goals of you and your partner. You must talk about the different things you wish to accomplish in your life and how those things will affect your relationship. Supporting the dreams of your partner and your partner supporting your goals is an essential part of having a sild marriage. Besides, what a better motivator to succeed than the support of the one you love?

The next thing you must talk about is money and the spending habits each of you has. This discussion includes any debt you or your partner may have as well as your saving plans. However, if you have different spending habits it doesn't mean that your marriage is going to fail as long as your responsibilities are taken care of and there is money left for you to be comfortable.

Another discussion you need to have before tying the knot is whether you want children or no as well as when you should have them. Starting a family should be a common decision and a general plan should be discussed before marriage. By getting married it doesn't necessarily mean that your partner wants to have children, so before making more wedding plans keep in the back of your mind that you should also pop up this question too. Also, you shouldn't have to agree on how many children you want just yet.

You should also talk about the past each of you had and the important things that affected your life. Like it or not, your past played a big role on who you are today and the same principle applies to your partner too. It doesn't matter that there are things in your past you are ashamed of. Your partner surely has some too and it will not hinder him or her from telling you about it. This discussion should include the existence of any previous spouses or children that may come from this previous marriage.

Also, you should talk about how each other response to stressful situations. Your partner may have seen how you react to stress since they have lived with you for a while, but hearing you talk about it as well as giving away some useful tips will be an added bonus to building your solid marriage. Many marriages end up in divorce because stressful situations have not been dealt with effectiveness that comes from effective communication.

It would be good to discover how to talk to each other. Not through emails, phones, or texts because your most important conversations as a married couple will occur through face to face contact. Any uncomfortable conversations you will have will be dealt with accordingly and with effectiveness if you have cleared beforehand how each partner faces various serious problems. You don't only have to talk about how you should speak to each other through difficult situations, you could only talk about the various habits you have when communicating that gets on each other's nerves or love.

Another thing you should do before getting married to the one you love is to live with him or her. This way you will be able to see which are the habits your partner has that will annoy you the most and deal with them before things get out of hand. There are many traits your partner will have that you will find out during that time and may annoy you too much for you to be able to handle. There have been many reports of couples constantly arguing about small habits that have been an integral part of their partner's lives when they lived alone. The key here is compromise. When we live with someone else, we should take into consideration the things that annoy him or her and try to fix them. Just like your partner should do about the things that will annoy you.

If you re both working, then it should be wise to have a discussion about dividing up the chores of your house. You wouldn't want your house to be constantly a mess because neither partner will be too tired to tide up the place. Even if you think that dividing the chores is not a serious matter, you will find out that there will be arguments later because you didn't take out the trash and your house smells. So, try to fair and help each other out when it comes to house chores because this could potentially be a source of argument.

Another thing you should do before getting married is to plan a big trip together. Whether you believe it or not this trip will be a source of stress for both of you since you will have to book a hotel room and plane tickets as well as organize your budget for this trip. This will be a perfect exercise that will somewhat show you how to handle your future shared responsibility. Also, when you reach your destination, you will have to make various decisions on where to go, what to do while you are there, and where you should spend your money. A trip will be a true eye opener.

When you are getting married to someone the most essential thing you will need to accept and realize is that you will share a future you will create together, you will have a common purpose. If you want different things, you will never be able to unite so as to achieve this common purpose.

However, if you have successfully managed to plan a future together, you will have to make compromises, deal effectively with the various problems that will arise through effective communication and share your thoughts with your partner. Be honest and true to your significant other and do not take advantage of his or her love for you. A solid marriage will make you the happiest person in the world if it is treated with the respect it deserves.

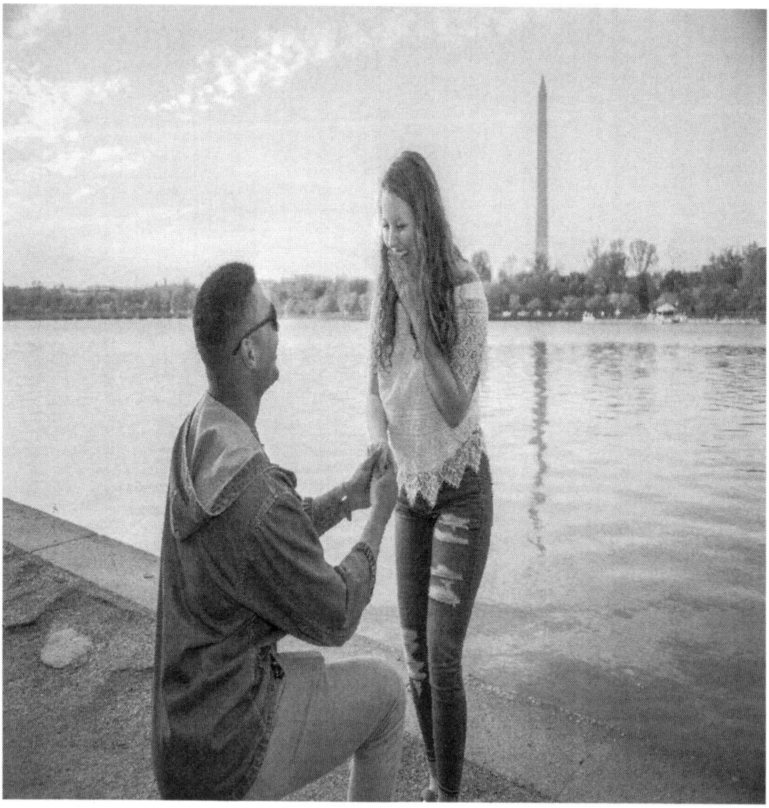

CHAPTER 23:

Creating a Higher Sense of Intimacy with Your Partner

Now, when we are talking about intimacy here, we need to understand that we are not talking just about sex. While sex is an vital part of a healthy relationship, and should be something that you can discuss comfortably, and consider with your partner on a regular basis as your sexual desires and needs change over time, it is important to remember that there are other forms of intimacy that need to be focused on in order to help your relationship grow stronger and your relationship to stay around.

By the way, it's important that we speak to a large extent on sexual communication, how it helps to build your relationship and avoid insincerity from any party. Partners in a relationship who fail to bring up matters on sex may be due to them seeing it as a lesser topic for deliberation, or it doesn't seem pleasant to them, is at a risk of some kind. It is important to question your partner of your lapses and where you've to make amends. It shouldn't piss you off or cause a disagreement. It is a route to building a reliable and lasting relationship.

Sexual communication is expected to be at the peak of topics for discussion in every relationship that aims to grow stronger and longer. This creates a balancing ground for partners and shaves off distrust of any kind. It is no doubt that a huge number of persons find it absurd or, less important to discuss sex with their partners whenever they feel sober or unsatisfied. They feel the best is to consult a third party, whether through books, findings made through the internet or their friends or relatives, they find comfort from this discussion and sought remedies, this is done with the total exclusion and awareness of their partner.

Why should there even be a sexual communication in the first place? Sexual communication is so cogent that it must not be sidelined in any relationship. It has a way of building the sensation that creates a strong bond, it makes partners share the innermost part of themselves which invariably makes them share other parts of themselves, intrinsic or extrinsic troubles. You should not be ashamed of letting your partner know where he needs to make amend. "Oh, the styles are cool, do make a readjustment here", the mode at which this discussion should be made must be on a polite and frank note, you can do the jokes but with a sincere face, let them know what bothers pertaining their sexual activities.

Therefore, how then do we make this sexual communication on a simple note, concise, conservative and with honesty? The steps are as follows:

1. Do not bring up this topic after having sex: You know that moment when the truth hurts, when it might not be so easy to bear, that is the period. You should not bring up matters related to the sex you made abruptly, it demeans your partner sense of humor and it could result into a misunderstanding. When is suitable to bring up the matter for ironing? It could come later during your bedtime or when there's an outing involving just the two of you but not immediately after the sex.

2. Do not make your conversation on sex seem like a shock to the partner: This is very much important, there are times to convey your message and it will be swiftly understood. You

should try to present these matters in a happy atmosphere. You should endeavor not to speak the truth that may destabilize your partner when you unleash his shortfalls. The conversation that has deepened the interest of your partner is an open space to let them know. It'll make them know of the need to fill the loopholes and connect those pleasures you want to feel during your sexual intercourse.

3. A quiet place far from home: There is a possible case of not having a quiet time with your partner. Tight work schedule, children frolicking, and the chores at home gives you no time for your partner. Make a quiet time. Maybe somewhere far from home where the children are far from earshot. This quiet place is an opportunity for both partners to reminisce on their sexual life. You can talk on when you both first had sex, this will then extend into discussing your present situation. Do you feel the warmth as much as you felt during your first night? Do you feel that absolute pleasure during sex or has it deflated? Do you feel that wondrous sensation that looks unquenchable or it has started to fade? These and many more are what you can talk on during this quiet time.

4. Present it in the form of a suggestion: The erratic behavior of people to when sexual discourse is brought for discussion that nails them to a fault makes it so difficult for partners to anger their beloved. This is why you must present it in the form of a suggestion. This won't all the time sound embarrassing or seen as a means to belittle him. Your choice of words must be cautiously chosen so as not to arouse their anger.

If you adhere to the enlisted ways, it will help you enormously in bringing up sexual matters with your partner. If you feel you are enclosed in thoughts pertaining to your sex life because you're trying to maintain the relationship, the harbored thoughts will further lessen your strength and leave you in shatters. Therefore, ponder on every word herein, muster that heart to bring up matters of your sexual life with your relationship and you shall have more than one cause to enjoy a lasting relationship. To reiterate, relationship that sidelines sexual communication is open to seismic disruption. Love them but most importantly talk about your sexual life with your partner.

How do you control your partner if they react badly?

Sexual communication should not sprout any bit of quarrel, but it should rather be a basis to build a comforting relationship lay on honesty, understanding, openness, and love. The above phase that talked on when and the appropriate time and place to bring up matters that relate to your sexual life with you partner will also tremendously help us in treating reaction too. For example, the quiet place that was proposed, if they react disorderly, you are in the position to put them in order. Make them know the importance of your sexual life and why they need to give ears to your suggestion.

Sex can't be completely separated from a relationship and a relationship that never bothers on the pleasure derived by the partners is most likely not last long. You must be able to bring joy to yourself if you can face your partner and let them know the importance of sex in modifying the mightiness of your union.

In building your intimacy through other means, to start with, we are going to talk about the five methods that you need to follow in order to create some more emotional intimacy with your partner. Emotional intimacy allows you and your partner a way to not only look good on paper, and to the outside world, but also to look good on the inside. It allows you both to know each other deeply, in a way that no one else should know you or your partner.

The good news is that this intimacy can be obtainable, no matter how long you have been in the relationship. Provided that both of you are willing to invest the time being vulnerable, and you are willing to talk to each other, you can make this work. Some of the steps that you can follow to create a deeper sense of intimacy between you and your partner includes:

When you start the conversation, pick out safer topics

When you first get started, you don't want to just jump into the tough stuff. Even if you have been into the relationship for a long time, jumping into the deep stuff can be intimidating, and can make one or both of you feel nervous and unsure of how you should proceed. Starting with some of the safer topics, the ones that you are both pretty sure how the other one is going to respond can be a much better option. This allows you to feel more comfortable, to get the hang of the process, and can build up some confidence for when you get deeper into this process.

So, to start, you need to focus your conversation. You can choose to do this for a few months or any length of time that you would like. Make sure that you set aside a good 30 minutes a day to talk and work on this. And when you start, you want to make sure that you are working with some comfortable topics so that this activity is more enjoyable, and you will be more willing to stick with it for the long term.

There are a lot of questions that you can talk to your partner about with this in mind. You can ask them about some of the memories that they remember back from when you were dating and ask why that memory is so important to them. Ask if there is something that they would love to be able to go back and do again.

Make it clear that both partners can share anything

When you are working on these conversations, make sure that both parties know that anything is safe to say or share during this time. Starting out with these conversations can be hard, but when everyone knows that they are in a safe space then they may be more willing to go along with it. You and your partner both want what is best for one another, so why try to make the other one feels bad or feels worried about what is going on when they tell you something?

This isn't an excuse for one or the other to be mean to each other. You can't go into this and say all of the bad things that your partner has ever done wrong in the relationship. This isn't going to be productive, and can make it almost impossible for them to feel good or open up to you. This is supposed to be a time for the two of you to learn more about each other, and to gain a fuller knowledge about one another. If one of the partners feels like they are being attacked, then they aren't going to open up, and they will probably try to get out of doing this again.

The point here is for the conversation to be a good way for you and your partner to become vulnerable with each other. This is the only way that the two of you are going to become more intimate with each other in this sense of the word. If you aren't opening up the floor as a safe space, then it is going to be almost impossible to get any further.

CHAPTER 24:

Marriage Secrets

When it comes to getting married, there are only a few people who are certain what they are getting themselves into. The truth is that we all have an idea of what marriage is about. What we have are hopes, expectations, and dreams of what marriage truly looks like. When we watch some of the movies starts we like, we think that the kind of marriages they show on Tv is what it is like in real life.

Well, let me tell you something, you have no idea what marriage is until you are there!

When I was getting married to my wife, there are things that I thought I knew, but once I got in, that is when I got the real deal! Getting married does not also mean that you will know everything. However, you will get to learn new things as you get by.

Here are some of the secrets I can tell you will strengthen your marriage if you pay attention to them;

Secret 1 Marriage is more about intimacy than sex

If you ask anyone that is single and planning to get married what marriage is about, they will tell you it is about sex. While there is so much value you draw from getting married to your partner as far as your sexual relationship, the truth is that a good marriage is built on intimacy. This is the only way you are going to enjoy good sex and not the other way around.

When I got married, I was excited that we were finally going to enjoy all the sex we want with my partner, and we do! However, I never quite understood the concept of real intimacy until I committed to spending the rest of my life with my lovely wife. What I have come to learn and understand is that marriage is a brilliant opportunity in which you allow your partner to look right inside your life, heart, and mind. That is what true intimacy is about!

Secret 2 Marriage uncovers self-centeredness but also cultivates selflessness

Confessions, I didn't realize how selfish I was until I got married to my wife. One year down the line, my selfishness was out in the light. I could choose what restaurant we would eat, who gets to clean up, what movie we will watch, and who gets the remote. What was even shocking was that each time we argued, my wife would apologize first even if I was the one at fault.

One thing you need to realize about marriage is that if you are going to make it last, you have to learn to place the needs of your spouse before your own. This is how you start learning the true meaning of being selfless. Trust me, even though this is a hard lesson to learn, it is a beautiful reminder of God's selflessness when He gave His all so that you and I can have it all in abundance.

Secret 3 Oneness means being ONE

Have you taken a time to think about the spiritual and physical benefits of oneness? The truth is that most people fail to consider the part where it is slightly inconveniencing, living in one house, sleeping on one bed, sharing the same bathroom, working with the same budget, and operating one bank account, among others.

The truth is, when we get into marriage, we stop being "me" and become "us." We stop having things that are "mine," and we view everything as "ours." To build a healthy relationship, you have to care for everything as though they were not just yours but also belonged to the person that you love most.

Secret 4 At certain points, you will be disappointed

This is one of the most tough realities that most couples find it hard to believe. You must be aware of your spouse's humanity and yours too. However, it is interesting that this reality does not hit home sooner until you are disappointed.

My wife and I have always loved each other deeply. This does not mean that we have not hurt each other a few times in our relationship. One thing you have to set in mind is that when you marry someone, you are choosing to bury your heart in theirs, and theirs in yours.

What you need to be ready for is that there will come a day when you will feel an ache. This agony can come in the form of an unkind word, a selfish moment, or even a thoughtless action. However, you must choose to embrace the grace of God so that every hurt and wound pave the way for forgiveness and restoration. Each wound should serve as a constant reminder of our need to love deeply and better each time.

Secret 5 You must learn the meaning of forgiveness whether you like it or not

The fact that you are going to get hurt means that you have to embrace the reality of learning the essence of forgiveness. One lesson that you must learn is that forgiveness comes not just because your partner deserves it, but because it whelms from a heart that understands how much forgiveness we had received even when we least deserved it.

Secret 6 Marriage will cost you

When you are in the glory of marriage, the truth is that you will lose a part of yourself. In other words, you exchange a portion of who you are for the sake of taking up a little bit of who your partner is. In short, you learn the essence of giving and taking. In marriage, you will know to let go of the things that do not matter to you at all. What you realize eventually is that what you have given is far much less than what you receive ultimately.

Trust me; love is good, just like that!

Secret 7 Love is a series of decision and not a feeling

Before you got married, the chances are that you did not understand the strong feelings that you felt. And then, suddenly, you start realizing that you cannot trust your feelings because there are days when you don't like your spouse, and most days, you just can't let him go.

Note that feelings are temporary. They come and go. They are more like a compass, and in other instances, they serve as a guide, but the truth is that you cannot follow them because they don't lead anywhere specific.

The true test of love is what you do when you feel that you don't like your spouse. Understand that marriage is about choosing to love your partner even when you don't want to. You are choosing to give your all into serving them because you committed to them, the world, and God that you would love them "for better or for worse." It is about you constantly choosing your spouse instead of yourself.

That is what true life means!

Secret 8 Marriage requires that you learn how to communicate

We have mentioned before that one of the most important building blocks of marriage is effective, clear, and honest communication with each other. It does not matter what it is that you are fighting about with your spouse. What matters the most is what you would do about it. How you will choose to communicate to them how you feel.

In short, marriage is about you constantly communicating with your spouse, your values, beliefs, opinions, and feelings. It is about not fearing to ask the tough questions, tell the hard truth, or even respond to difficult questions. It serves as a lifeline between you and your spouse. Trust me; there is no other way around it. You have to be ready to take responsibility for what you say, how you say it, and how you react to your partner's response.

Watch your tone, sarcasm, and body language! It speaks a lot.

Secret 9 Marriage is not the end of your destination

When you are still dating, it is often easy to look at marriage as your grand finale! It is that thing that you have been dreaming about since you were a little girl or boy. It is what you have lived for all your life, and finally, it is here. The next thing you think of when you get married is, "Now what?"

What you need to discern is that the relationship and marriage God has blessed you with is just a small portion of the grand scheme he has set for your life. The truth is that your purpose and passion will supersede the relationship you have with your partner. God will use your relationship and the love between you and your spouse for the glory of His name.

Your marriage is not the end of everything. Instead, it is just the beginning of the many more blessings he has in store for you.

So, quit giving up and fixing your mind on an ending. He has so much up his sleeve, and you have not seen anything yet!

Secret 10 Marriage offers you a glimpse of so much more

Aside from the fact that you already know God has so much more in store for you, there is a lot you have to learn about God as you interact with other people regularly. Realize that there is a reason why God uses the institution of marriage when talking about the love He has for the church.

There is no single relationship you are going to have that will compare to that intimacy that is exchanged through marriage here on earth. The love that God has for us is magnified through the lens of a strong, healthy, and long-lasting marriage. But the best part is that he uses the institution of marriage to teach us, mold us, refine us, and laid us through the test. In other words, it is through marriage that God keeps making us be more of Him.

When we reflect on the love of God in the way we love our spouse, we honor Him, and that is exactly what He uses to keep our marriages alive. What you need to understand is that there are so many ways you can achieve holiness, and marriage is one of them. Note that you are a different person because of the relationship he has given you and realize that he is not yet finished with you. Always purpose to expect from Him every single day.

CHAPTER 25:

Dealing with Temptations

Every day we are faced with temptations. They can be anything from getting a new motorcycle to cheating. Anytime we are tempted to do something we know, we should not do it is a temptation.

For me, my biggest temptation is chocolate. Even though chocolate is not a serious offense in a marriage. Yet, it is still a temptation. The problem is, the way we deal with our temptations. If you have a chocolate temptation, let your spouse help you kick it. They will gladly hide it from you, so you cannot find it.

I remembered a few years ago, and I was craving chocolate. My wife does not allow me to have much, and so the craving is always here. I went to the store to get groceries and picked up some chocolate. I snuck it home and hid it under the bed. Little did I know she was cleaning the bedroom that day. The chocolate that was hiding was found. What a sad and depressing day. Chocolate is one thing, but what about temptations in your marriage? There are some severe temptations that you must avoid. I realize that you cannot stop your urge of attractions. The best solution is to run away.

The history of temptation goes back during pre-historic times. It is as old as, back to the Garden of Eden. The devil, in the form of a serpent, tempted the first humans, Adam and Eve. They fell for the lies the serpent told them. The Bible says a lot of stories about the temptation. It has always been a part of human nature to be tempted. Temptations are brought our curiosity; we indulge in things that entice us, gratify us, and makes us feel emotions we have not thought for a long time. Temptations come in several different ways, such as eating healthy foods, maintaining a good lifestyle, managing finances, and attraction to someone. There is a lot of ways to be tempted. In some context, the temptation is connected to sin for those who sinned are those that cannot resist temptation. The temptation may be used to the state of being satisfied without following moral standards.

The attraction is one way to be tempted, and perhaps the reason is why affairs and sexual intimacy to someone other than your partner are happening. Although it is reasonable to be attracted to other people, what matters is how you act on those feelings and how you stop it before it creates sin in the marriage.

In marriage, every affair begins with a temptation of an attraction. Marriages break up because one partner loses themselves in fascination and thinks they can get away with it. One selfish act can wipe out your relationship and vanish the years of integrity. Most families are broken caused by one of the parents having an affair and not thinking about what effects it may have.

In some cases, the notion of a marital affair will always lead to blaming the husband. In every cheating husband, there must also be a cheating woman. Extramarital relations outside marriage where an illicit romance or sexual relationship, romantic friendship or intimate attachment occurs are being done by two persons. An affair that carries on in one form or another for years will eventually lead to separation and divorce.

In a marriage concept, temptation often builds up when one partner started looking for someone who treats them better than their spouse. A marriage becomes weak when facing problems; for example, a wife becomes attracted to a man who empathizes and listens to her more. Both partners are susceptible to committing a mistake. Marital problems were existing between partners, and it has become easy to look for others who will give them the attention they are not getting from their spouse. It is a human weakness to fall for someone who gives them more attention and affection. Eventually, confiding their problems to that person will lead to closeness resulting in an affair.

The temptation is one of the challenges married couples are facing. Together, we will learn how to identify various ways on how to deal with temptation. You will learn the underlying factors that cause temptation to exist in your marriage and its consequences if it continues to exist. Each topic will provide you with solutions that refrain you from being tempted. However, this will only serve as a guide for married couples that are currently facing temptation as a challenge but not to the extent that would provide an exact solution to the matters at hand. Spouses need to keep an open mind when working out a marriage, it is not suitable for judging your spouse if they committed a mistake, but rather it will be helpful if you keep an open ear and trust them to be honest about their confession. Marriage is hard work, and making it successful takes a lifetime. It is only common for couples to experience temptation along the way; the important thing is to have both partners to be determined to drive against it.

Take the time to go over the list of ways on how to battle temptation. It will provide insights that can assist couples in determining ideas on how to overcome temptation. It is better to discuss this with your partner to be able to come up with a solution that could help you resolve your situation.

The Courage to Resist Temptation

Temptation can be described as an immediate pleasurable urge and impulse to fill the void of something lacking. It exists because something is lacking in a married couple's life. Some say affairs happen because the love of each spouse was no longer alive. It involves a romance that brings back those memories of being pursued, excitement, and sexually intimate. It makes you feel young and being wanted again.

One way to avoid temptation is to fill the void of whatever you feel is lacking in your relationship. Sometimes we compare our married life to others, and nowadays, with the use of technology, we often see the gaps in our relationship. We long for consistency of love, touch, romance, and the desire brought about by our insecurities, making ourselves more vulnerable to temptations. We try to think of scenarios of "what ifs." What if our husband is more compassionate than he is now, practices romance, and remembers all the special occasion? Then maybe we wouldn't be tempted to look for others in the first place. You try to picture a different person out of your husband throughout your marriage. You no longer admire the one you signed up for through marriage. We often believe that it is our husband's fault that you came looking for others, but it's not. Signing up for marriage is nothing like a membership club; you pay the fee and use it all you want. In marriage, you must make all the effort to keep your membership, or otherwise, you'll be taken out.

The critical thing to remember in resisting temptation is to have the "courage" to resist temptation. For instance, thinking of others through your thoughts during your marriage chaos, such as leaving your spouse or involving in an affair, will feel desirable at the moment; however, in the long run, it bears undesirable results. Exercising self-control is also essential; it makes us feel superior to our desires. Once we thought we are walking on the wrong path, we need to take a detour and regain control of ourselves. We need to paint the 'what will happen" if we succumb to temptation. Fixates ourselves to the aftereffects if we divulge on our selfish desires. We cannot sacrifice the well-being of our family. Giving in to temptation will result in a broken marriage and interfere with your long-term goals. We were making it easier to deal with temptation if you were avoiding what tempts you.

Do not Be Surprised When It Happens

Do not be afraid, but rather be prepared. Make it a habit dealing with temptation, for it's always there. Temptation can come in any form; for instance, your eating habits, sleeping routine, and managing your finances. Let us acknowledge that we will be tempted in all kinds somehow, but the upper hand of letting it happen is in our hands. You were born with the wisdom of differentiating what is wrong from right, and through this, we will be able to determine what is better.

You need to be prepared. Like commencing a "fire drill" in a school to make students and staff prepare in case, a real incident will happen. You must equip yourselves with the knowledge that is beneficial for you in dealing with temptations. For example, exposing yourself to healthy foods through the process of not buying processed or carb-filled food will take you to your goals of achieving a healthy lifestyle. You need to have the determination to continue what you are starting.

Giving in to temptation is only one part of the journey, but do not be surprised if you see yourself on the verge of losing it. Be prepared and regain your self-control.

Ask for help

People with a strong sense of independence are not fond of asking for help in times of trouble. They believe it is their responsibility to resolve problems on their own without asking for help. Most people think of a notion that temptation often leads to marital affairs. These stereotypes suppress people from talking about attractions. They don't want to be judged and make their family look as if they're breaking apart; therefore, keeping it from others. For some, the word temptation alone carries the burden history of a broken marriage and family. Most often, marital affairs are caused by temptation, such as husbands cheating on their wives or wives cheating on their husbands. The attraction had done its part in creating chaos in the married world. It is good to be aware of another way of dealing with temptation is to ask for help. It is significant to have someone that you can consult with the same experiences you have. Realizing that someone has gone through what you are also going through is like a breath of fresh air. Through your friends, you can ask for help. For example, the way you resist temptation in a particular situation. It's better to have someone who can understand where you are coming from and who will pay attention to your thoughts without judgment. Asking for help can have many benefits, such as helping you progress better and faster. Asking for help makes you feel more grateful, you develop your sense of trust, and strengthen your relationship to the people you confide in. You are bound to live with companions, which is where the famous saying "No man is an island" comes from. Everybody needs a companion or friend. It is not weakness to ask for help. If you choose to accept support from someone you can trust, they might teach you something new and provide you with more useful knowledge that you can use in your marriage.

COUPLE THERAPY

CHAPTER 26:

How to Live a Happy Relationship

Relationships require maintenance and constant work for it to succeed and turn into a long, loving, and happy relationship. People are often taught that love just happens, and sometimes they are even told that for a relationship to be successful, love is all that is needed. However, relationships are much more than that and love is not enough. Love can be the first spark that ignites the relationship and is how it came to exist. To build a long-lasting connection with another person, you need to think in more realistic terms when it comes to defining love. Expanding on the simplistic view, or fairytale, you dreamt of when you were young is the first step.

For a happy relationship, you have to actively work on it and make the best of everything you encounter on your path to happiness. Having a happy relationship means making conscious choices that will work towards that happiness, even if sometimes the decisions you make seem difficult and challenging.

Everyone makes mistakes when it comes to relationships, and we aren't referring to solely romantic ones. Even with friends, our behavior might influence how much they trust us, rely on us, and how much we will connect with them, and on what level. The fact we all make mistakes doesn't mean there is nothing you can do about it. There is actually a lot! There are procedures both you and your partner can take to avoid mistakes, manage them if they already happened, and bring happiness to your relationship:

1.   Your partner is your equal: This is something people often forget when they are bossing each other around. Do you recognize yourself or your partner while reading this? Instead of being the leader of the relationship, try collaboration. Work together, listen to your partner, and be as supportive as possible.

2.   Be respectful: Spending a lot of time with one person can be indeed exhausting, especially if you live with your partner. Once in a while, it may seem like your partner is triggering your nerves or anxiety, and you may feel anger or resentment building up. You may end up lashing out even if he or she isn't entirely at fault. No matter how you feel, how mad you are, your partner needs to learn about such emotions respectively. Communication plays an significant role here as well as self-control. Practice both of these even outside of your relationship, and you will see only the positive influence it leaves on people.

3.   Spend quality time with your partner: Back when your relationship was fresh and new, you spent so much time together, and you did everything together. Where did all of that go? Well, life happens, children come, people focus on their jobs and careers, home, chores, and so on. Some may lose all of their free time that they used to devote to their partners. Even so, for a relationship to succeed, you need to make that time even when it's scarce. Happy relationships demand you to push yourself and your partner and do something together. It is not enough to talk to each other at the end of the day about work or various problems. Quality time means getting to work together on a project. For instance, you can repaint your home, build a dollhouse for

your kids, go hiking or exercising together, volunteer in an animal shelter, and so on. By working together on something that you are both interested in, you will reconnect and even learn new things about each other. It is a satisfying and enriching experience.

4. Learn how to forgive: It is essential to know how to forgive your partner's mistakes, but you also have to be ready to forgive yourself. Empathy plays a significant role in forgiveness. It helps you feel your partner's emotions, understand their behavior, and make room in your heart for real and unconditional forgiveness. Be the same towards yourself. Learn self-compassion and practice it. It is a great skill that will not just heal wounds created by mistakes, but also teach you not to repeat them.

Confidence, Honesty and Loyalty

The three most desirable traits people seek in their love interests are confidence, honesty, and loyalty. But they do not come easily to everyone. Some gain them during their childhood, while others have to learn them and stay true to them to build a healthy, stable relationship.

Confidence

We quickly develop low self-esteem if you are hurt in a previous relationship. It may be hard to win back your trust, but it is not impossible. Confidence should be strong yet yielding, as overconfident people can be inflexible and bad listeners. However, the right amount will improve your relationship, the way you react in stressful situations, and it will positively affect your health. There is a series of exercises you could do every day to build your confidence, such as the following:

1. Imagine what you want to be: Visualizing your goals is a fantastic technique to build motivation. It will keep you moving and remind you of your aspirations and goals. Don't be afraid to talk about what you want with friends, family, and especially with your partner. They can help you get there, with proper advice or with support.

2. Affirm yourself: It means you need to vocalize positive statements and opinions regarding yourself. It may sound meaningless at first, but hearing it, even hearing yourself saying it out loud, will help you believe it. The human brain tends to accept statements more quickly if they are in the form of a question. Instead of saying, "I am good with money," try asking yourself, "why am I so good with money?"

3. Challenge yourself: Once a day, do something that scares you. In most cases, the best way to overcome fear is to face it. Anxieties often stop people from performing simple, everyday tasks like making a phone call, going to the bank, or meeting new people. Doing things that scare you will push you to realize that you can improve yourself. Going through the challenge may even boost your self-confidence and in time help you get over some of your anxieties. Just be sure to make a ritual of it and challenge yourself every day.

Honesty

Being honest is so much more than telling the truth. It also means not keeping any secrets from your partner, caring for others, and having integrity. Being honest means your partner can fully rely on you, trust you with his whole heart, and be proud of you. Take note, that even small "white" lies can generate relationship problems, mistrust, and anxiety, for yourself as well as your partner once he or she learns the truth. If you find yourself telling small lies due to your stress, you may need to practice honesty. Here are the steps you can take to learn how to be completely honest without being anxious:

1. Understand why you lied: Did you fabricate things to make yourself look better? Or to avoid embarrassment? Understanding why you lied is a big step forward to changing the things about you for the better. People lie for various reasons but being aware of those reasons will help you deal with them in other ways. Perhaps you need to work on your confidence, or you think you deserve more respect. Try to earn it with honesty instead of making up stories about yourself. People often lie out of shame or out of a lack of confidence and self-esteem. For instance, if you did something you aren't proud of, you may be tempted to cover it up with lies. Many people even lie to themselves in an attempt to get rid of that feeling of shame. Instead, be responsible and accept your bad behavior because acceptance allows you to take the steps needed to correct it. This way, you will show others that you can be honest and possibly someone to trust and rely on.

2. Change your behavior: Guilt is a powerful feeling, and any behavior that has led you to experience it will cause anxiety. When you are found guilty by others, you may also lose their respect. Being guilty and admitting it will more often bring understanding instead of judgment, especially when it comes to your partner who loves you. However, you should not rely on knowledge alone. Try to change bad habits and behaviors and avoid putting yourself in a situation that will make you feel guilty and that will make you lie to your loved ones.

3. Don't compare yourself to others: In our attempt to be better and earn respect, we often lie about who we are. You need to recognize who you are and to learn to live with it, even if you see yourself in a negative light. Don't forget that anxiety

often makes people overly critical of themselves, and you might not be as faulty as you think. Improve yourself, work on your personality, and become who you want to be instead of lying about it. Instead of making up things about yourself to impress your partner, let your honesty impress him. It will build a connection between the two of you, and it will make your relationship stronger.

4. Avoid lying for others: Sometimes, our friends and family will put us in stressful situations and ask us to lie for them. Let them know this is not an option for you and that you are an honest person. If they want you to keep a secret for them, be sure you can do it, and don't dive in to the temptation of gossip.

Loyalty

When we think about loyalty in a relationship, it usually means as not cheating. But, loyalty also implies devotion to your partner, being faithful, committed, and honest. Loyalty is so much more than just fidelity. It means opening yourself to your partner and sharing all of your emotions, thoughts, and opinions. Here's what you can do to show and prove your loyalty to your partner:

1. If you want to be truly loyal to your partner, you have to be honest with yourself. Practice transparency, get to know yourself and be aware of who you are. We often have the wrong image of ourselves, and if you don't know yourself, how could you offer to be connected to someone else. How can you share yourself, and commit?

2. Be open with your partner. Not just honest but let them read you. Share your emotions and opinions at the end of your day. Sit down with your partner and spend time talking about

your day. Include all the events and express how it made you feel and how it has influenced you.

3. Don't put yourself in the position that will make you hide something from your partner. Don't hide events, experiences, and don't hide your emotions. Keeping secrets is postponing the inevitable. Secrets will somehow come out one way or another and your attempt to hide them will just cause pain for you and your partner.

4. Be supportive. Be present for your partner through the good and bad. We all have our moments when even the slightest tantrum will trigger anxiety. Don't judge your partner. Don't tell him or her how to behave or what to do. Support them with understanding and care. Don't say things like "There is no reason to be angry", say it "I understand why that would make you angry."

CHAPTER 27:

Overcoming Negative Thinking

All sorts of things can ruin a perfectly successful relationship. For example, money and incompatibility are the two big ones. But according to professionals there is one thing that can destroy a relationship more than anything else. Nicole Issa Psy. D., a Bustle certified psychologist calls it "the ultimate relationship killer", that is, negative thinking! There's a very close feedback loop between the thoughts, emotions, and actions of a person. And getting negative thoughts will take you down the rabbit hole." It's important to realize that your habits of thinking will contribute to major relationship issues. Early childhood encounters with your parents, for example, can lead you to believe you're unworthy of love. Because of that, you may go into a relationship believing that at some point, your partner will abandon you, and you may be afraid to speak up.

The truth is we're making our own truth. When we assume we have a good relationship, then we work through things hoping everything will always be fine. But when you enter a relationship with pessimistic feelings, you always expect the worst not only of your partner but of the result of your relationship.

You'd like to think twice before you let yourself down or place an over-negative and frustrating relationship if you're looking for love (like most of us). When you are trying to find true friendship or the right relationship, you're going to want to be more optimistic about your approach. Meaning: you're going to have to be more optimistic about your spouse, particularly if it's fresh, and you're going to want to be more open-minded to love and be real, when you know how much you value. If you start to put in fear, doubt, hesitation, and a false character, you'll probably lose out on something that could be awesome down the road.

Will negative thinking ever harm you? You know some signs firsthand whether you're harshly critical or trapped in concern, stress, anxiety, depression or low self-worth. Negative thinking can affect our relationships, our health and our jobs, our lives, intensely and often devastatingly.

I think everyone can break free from negativity for good with the four keys mentioned below. Why do I think so? And if I can (and I have) from the dark place in which I used to be, I believe those resources will also work for you — wherever you are.

People also seek and get rid of their negative ideas in several different ways including distraction. They 'drink their sorrows' and later and punish themselves emotionally for still being trapped in their misery. It could feel like a true inner struggle. These are common policies that seek in the short run to stop the thoughts and relieve the pain, but which only exacerbate things in the long term. The question at its root is not solved.

The work shows that challenging, contending, attempting to overwhelm or push unhelpful thoughts just amplifies and worsens issues.

I work with clients to find satisfaction in their relationships as a professional wellness coach, of course, you must express the good and evil in terms of thoughts and feelings while you are honest so that your partner is better equipped to do all that.

But it might be too much to deal with if you're ever bitter or pissed off, particularly if you know it's too long or too lengthy.

Moreover, you should not only be thinking negative thoughts about a potential relationship but also the negative thoughts that might keep you from putting yourself in the first place. You will not give yourself a reasonable chance to find love and match with someone when there are too much strain and doubt. The crap? Know when to hold negative feelings in order to boost mental wellbeing and when to make those unpleasant thoughts constructive.

Think of other times they've taken some time to react or prove. This shows that they're still interested. The alternative idea here could be straighter than just because I haven't even heard of them yet, that doesn't mean they're not interested.

Recall that controlling your goals is important to your relationship's success. In the world of relationships, discord and conflict are inevitable, just note this is normal and all right. What is most important is how you and your partner manage and develop in tough times.

Recall that your partner is also a person. Not all your partner does will be "right" or "good," but you do not feel frustrated to put your critical lens on. Say your needs and do not want to spread the word when the entire relationship is hurt. Find the partner deliberately in a favorable light. Thank your partner for their little acts and deeds of love and kindness. Say thank you. This perpetuates your relationship with a supportive and caring loop.

Don't actually take it all. Poor dates, challenges, rough talks and times can be frustrating at the time. Don't add these experiences to the negative stack, but then find the life lessons that are aligned with your goals. Engage yourself to be happy on the journey to love.

Break up is not a viable option, whatever your toxic thinking is, it typically comes from the same position – fear. Fear of your partner quitting, in particular. When you [commit], I use an example, you burn the ship. You so honestly do not have a way to reach the island when you burn the ships, and you need to work together to survive. You should often see the positivity in every condition when there is no other choice. You will enable your relationship to come from a position of love rather than misery if you take the possibility of breaking out of the equation (i.e. 'burning your ship.'). It is easier for you to remain optimistic when your words and acts come from a position of affection. A thought is just thinking at the end of the day. It's not the truth, actually. Your connection will be a much stronger one if you don't allow it to overtake you.

Dr. Natalie Feinblatt, a licensed clinical psychologist, explains via email with Bustle, that he only need someone that's complete. You must love yourself and feel whole as if you want to open up to someone else. You are already done! There are two half-ways to form a whole, and there are two whole communities together to create a beautiful couple that is the basis for a lasting stable relationship.

This attitude generates a strong assumption that an individual is right for you. You certainly do not want anything to lose, this idea places incredible pressure on yourself to find the one thing and protect it. This might also make people choose partners who do not suit their wishes, since they are too overwhelming to release someone who may be one.

It's not going to work out. Don't get upset without understanding first even your date. In a new partnership, assuming it's like the last one (which obviously was a failure) gives the new relationship a ticking time bomb. This new relationship. Fear it and be hopeful instead.

It isn't like my husband. No similarities with a husband-boyfriend in your relationship or your spouse. Just don't do it. Just don't do it. Such things obviously aren't fit for you two anyway, they're different men. If you equate your relationship with one that has not been established in the past, then the relationship you are creating may be a failure. So sit tight and enjoy the magic and joy oozing out from your relationship. Give your partner an open and equal chance.

You can limit your chance of happiness by defining the ideal partner based on assumptions or personal preferences. He or she may prove to be the most affectionate and marvelous companion. It's not my kids. You might be shocked at the kind of person you ultimately fall in love with. Allow yourself to learn from someone you know and understand that there is no "kind" here.

You're going to cheat on me, is one way these thoughts could be fused in your head. If you've been lied on in the past, you may develop a presumption that all people cheat. This induces anxiety, leading to behaviors that stress and strain those involved. We should prevent mistrust, lack of contact and anxiety of involvement.

If this is the right guy, your true self will never get rid of it. "I'll mess this connection up." It just implies that it didn't work out and you're both not compatible. Breakdowns, as they arise, are the reason for new development. If the relationship is not meant to go on, it will become obvious. Do not repress the real and genuine self because it will only come out later anyway. Be safe. Be confident. Make moves.

"You're out of my own league." If you're constantly questioning your own values, you could ruin a relationship that is great. There wouldn't be any truthful partner left for you due to your lack of self-confidence. It also brings into question their decision by being with you first and foremost. Moreover, a poor partner sees this as a chance to step all over you.

You cannot change the people; instead, while in some areas, such as communication, you could create some improvements, you should take your partner for their core values. (They're not going anywhere.) Nobody wants to be a pet project. You're going to find that the next person that embraces them as they are is taking the whole job that you've done to make them the person you'd want to be. On the other hand, if they've never changed, you're frustrated with no reason.

If you constantly think that you are used for your money, power, or access, it's hard to know the real person, because you are likely to put up emotional walls to shield yourself and avoid an actual link. It protects you from getting hurt by putting up emotional walls, but it also protects you from getting love.

Some couples bring this into their marriages or relationships. "You would have done this or that if I meant anything to you." However, the truth is, don't expect too much from your relationship. Of course, empathy and consideration will be required when appropriate but you can ruin everything if you are too protective and demanding if it's not appropriate and you force others to be there too much for your every need. Taking it seriously is the end of the relationship. This also doesn't mean they don't value you if your loved one doesn't respond in the way you think you're supposed to or do something you won't do.

Don't worry about the ex of your partner. This doesn't matter. While it's in human nature to be curious about who our partners dated and even compete with them, it doesn't do anything positive just to waste time. Their ex is for a reason — it doesn't work! Forget about the past because it's not important at all today, the more time you waste thinking about their past relationships, the less time you have to make sure your present relationships work out. The most frustrating thing about this is that it sparks up insecurity in your mind and nothing is just enough to make you happy.

CHAPTER 28:

Tips and Strategies to Maintain Your Emotional Wellbeing

Reminders of Your Own Mental Health

There's no five-step program of fixing depression or your relationship. Depression is common in the short term, inevitable, and impacts everyone differently. You are likely to come across problems linked to it. Your outlook does, however, influence both your partnership and your ability to support your partner.

You are not their therapist. It's really important to show your love and support for your friend, but it is never equal to counseling or professional help for mental wellness. Don't put pressure on yourself to repair your partner's depression, because it's not your job. You are not liable for their hardships, and feeling as though you were places undue pressure on your relationship. Just do anything you need to support them, as would any committed friend.

You need self-care, and you may know that you are exhausted from constant high emotions. It's vital to care for your mental health. Many partners will overplay the needs of their significant others who are distressed. This may deplete your mental resources, and may even physically tax you. Take a step back and ensure you still have the support you need.

Empathy and open communication are important in all relationships, but when coping with depression, extra effort is needed. Depression in your relationship allows you to develop a new vocabulary of emotion with your partner.

Be transparent with how you feel, and realize that they can struggle to put their feelings into words. Validate what they're doing, even though you may not personally understand what they mean.

It's difficult to negotiate a relationship with a depressed partner. Depression will show relationship's defects and make them even more difficult to surmount. Many of the abilities needed, such as empathy, can, therefore, enhance any relationship.

How to help your partner when their anxiety is out of balance

1) Ask questions and do the best to understand what they are going through; it can be different for everyone. Some people will experience painful body reactions like a churning stomach or a heart rate out of control.

Although you can read articles online about what it is like to deal with anxiety, you won't get the full picture of your partner's reality.

It is a personal and profoundly subjective experience.

If you want to comprehend what it's like for them, you need to talk about it with them.

It's easier to have the conversation in a quiet room while you're home. After all, the friend needs to feel comfortable thinking about something that puts them in distress.

Here are three relevant questions you can ask:

a) Is there something about your anxiety you want me to know?

b) Is there something I can do that will help if you feel anxious?

c) Is there anything you might not like me to do?

As someone who has spent my entire life coping with anxiety, I can assure you it is not easy to talk about anxiety.

So be patient, and take your time talking with your partner about this difficult subject.

Note, you don't have to understand everything there is to know about your partner's anxiety, in one conversation. It'll take quite some time.

Also, if you've just started dating, it will probably take time to build the trust and understanding required to be completely truthful with each other about these kinds of things.

2) Do not underestimate the power of insight.

It is very normal for most anxious people not to want to speak about it.

If this is the case, even though they aren't transparent about it, by watching them in various circumstances, you can still learn a lot about your partner.

See how they are responding to other issues. Remember how awkward or relaxed they feel.

When you are closely watching, you will be able to grasp what is causing their fear, and what is not.

This is an immense support to your friend because they may not be able to communicate their fear.

The more you appreciate your mate, the more support they experience in the relationship.

This is what it takes to build a satisfying and long-lasting relationship.

3) Have patience.

Patience, when you're dating someone with anxiety, is a very important quality. Feeling antsy and trying to always be "in the know" will make things worse.

Unfortunately, being cautious often is the only option, particularly if your partner then experiences anxiety. Anxiety requires time to pass.

The important thing about anxiety that you need to realize is that it can't be "fixed."

Sure, some strategies and medications can help manage anxiety, but no one can be magically cured of their anxiety.

Instead of trying to save the day when your friend feels distressed, it's best to be patient and reassure them that everything is all right.

In reality, rushing to act will intensify your partner's anxiety. This is going to demonstrate to them that there is a major issue that will make their anxiety worse.

The best you can do is be cool, compassionate, and let them know you're with them.

4) Communicate with your partner clearly. Not being truthful with your partner will make matters worse. It will lead them to doubt what is going on and to see themselves second-hand.

That is not what an anxious person wants.

You need to communicate clearly and be sure in yourself.

This also means you should not be playing games. After you have seen it, don't take 4 hours to answer a message.

Be prompt and truthful, and respond when you see it.

It's about getting rid of unknowns.

Most anxiety is fear of what will happen in the future, so you can help your partner from second-guessing the future and themselves by being transparent and optimistic about what is going to happen.

5) Calm down. This one is very clear. If you get frustrated, nervous, or impatient, it won't support anyone with anxiousness.

Trust me when I say a person with anxiety likes to be around calm people.

You should aim to maintain your composure, particularly in moments of anxiety that your partner experiences.

It's also significant to note that anxiety can make you feel a little angry or rude to your partner. Sometimes, they do not want to speak with you. You must remain cool, calm, and composed in these situations.

Now, of course, if your partner abuses you while they feel anxiety, it shouldn't be accepted, and you need to talk about it with them.

But if they only want time to have space, you can give them that until their negative feelings have passed.

6) Don't presume that all the negative things in their lives originate from anxiety. Because anxiety is a major issue in

your partner's life, it can be normal to conclude that all the negative things originate from their mental state.

This just is not the case.

The fact is, we're all human, and all of us have our struggles.

It is easy to conclude that everything stems from anxiety but that does little to help your partner cope with what they are going through.

Know it's important to reach out. Take the time to consider what happens to your friend. Believe them.

7) Don't try to justify to them why they shouldn't be afraid of anything. Anxious people realize their fear is not logical. They know that what they are thinking about probably will not happen.

One thing to try is just thinking over what the worst-case scenario could be. This puts it out there and may even help them to know it's not that bad, really.

The most important thing is, don't make them fun for it. They know it how it sounds.

8) Understand that your partner might be nervous about the relationship for various reasons. This is not the case with everyone, but your partner might spend more time than other people thinking about things that may go wrong in the connection.

This is simply called "anxiety about relationships."

Here are some cases of what could be of interest to them:

"What if my anxiety breaks the relationship?"

"What if they cheat?"

"What if he / she's not going to reply to the text?"

"What if someone else likes them more?"

Now, don't get me mistaken: from time to time, most people have these feelings. That is natural. But nervous people may have certain thoughts or doubts more often than normal.

It can lead to greater physical discomfort and anxiety symptoms.

These troubling thoughts could lead an anxious partner to try to find out if their thoughts are real.

For instance, if they believe they are always the one who initiates a meeting first, they may ghost you for a couple of days to see if that is true.

They question their religions to see whether they are wrong or not. This increased stress may also lead to angry or irritable moods or evasive or passive behavior.

9) Do not take it personally.

Because anxiety is a harmful emotion, it can be normal for nervous people to take it out on other people sometimes.

If this turns into violence, then you will have a conversation about it with them.

But if you notice that they are often a little moody and have a go at you, don't take it personally. It is not about you. It is just about the fear they experience.

When you take it personally, then it will turn into an argument or a fight, and it will not do anything for anybody.

Know their bad mood is just temporary. They will be back to being their nice and fun-loving self in no time.

13) Do not look down on your partner.

Yes, it is necessary to show respect and compassion. But you're not meant to look down on your friend, and hate them.

It doesn't make them feel good, nor does it do anything for you. For example, if you're dating a chubby girl, make sure that you give her respect.

Yeah, they're nervous, but that doesn't make them worse than you are. We all have our problems, and while some people have more challenging struggles than others, no one deserves to be looked down on.

It's easier to consider your partner as your equal for the partnership. This is what they would like.

Understand that they are doing their hardest to cope with their fear, and in no way do they want to be handled differently. They want to be a regular person, so treat them as one.

14) Live your life well.

Most importantly, it hurts to see your partner endure pain and suffering. That's one of the hardest things to watch.

But you must continue living your life. They don't want to be the reason you don't live life to its fullest. This adds to the pressure that they are already going through.

What they desire is for you to live life and achieve your potential.

CHAPTER 29:

How and Why to Protect Each Other

The knack to communicate well the needs and feelings of each spouse makes the marriage a good one. After all, once we understand and cherish ourselves, we are better able to express ourselves. And for this reason, happy couples stay authentic, vulnerable, as well as honest with one another, in meeting their individual needs.

So, if your marriage experienced a slump for one reason or another, you should do your best to make it great again. And this can be done by learning the communication secrets of a joyful, harmonious, and symbiotic relationship. Technically speaking, these are happiness tips that can mutually benefit couples.

Being Mindful of your Spouse at All Times

Practicing mindfulness can be instrumental in cultivating and sustaining a healthy bond with your loved one. This can strengthen your ability to become present with your partner, which increases your mutual feelings of love and joy. Also, it enables you to be extra aware of the suffering your partner may be going through.

This awareness makes you less prone to overreact whenever the spouse acts from an area of suffering. When you can maintain mindfulness during those moments your partner is hurting, you will be far more inclined and capable of supporting them when they need it most. Ensuring your partner feels supported and loved is important for the harmony within your relationship.

Effectively and Regularly Communicating

This is quite obvious and its importance is impossible to exaggerate in relationships. Completely disclosing and paying attention to the reasons for the suffering of each other is the solitary way to fix the differences among couples. Listening is vital because over and over again we spend so much time attempting to show our opinion that we neglect to recognize, besides eliminate, the behaviors that perpetuate the suffering of our partner.

Also, effective communication allows us to make sure that we hold a firm picture of reality. And this will cause our decisions not to be founded on the false-negative tales that we tell ourselves from time to time.

Willingness to Adapt as Needed

Change and growth are inevitable within healthy relationships. While people all understand that growth cannot occur without facing the unknown, the majority are deathly uneasy with adjusting. This discomfort leads people to react with only two choices: either fight the partner or run away. When we react by this mode, we lose our chance to bring accord into our bond. Hence, we must admit that relationships change. By staying mindful, we can remain calm and find out the best mode to adjust to change.

Sustaining Perspective

Maintaining an outlook on the meaning of our disparities is important. Once we lack this attitude, an insignificant distinction has the makings to turn into something very significant. To avoid this from happening, we must ask ourselves all the time if the problem is sufficiently important to cause a conflict. Often, we are better off taking our spouse as himself or herself than making a case over anything superfluous to the wellbeing of our marriage. It is far easier to sustain agreement in our relations when we skip arguing over the small stuff.

Fostering Freedom

When single, we have the full direction of our existence. Upon deciding to share your life with someone, however, both parties need to give up this concept of control. After all, when one person commands all features of the relations, the other will feel browbeaten. Oppression is untenable over the long run because people in due course resent their deficiency of freedom. When we commit to share our life with someone, each spouse must give the other a choice to respect the wishes of the other.

Love Rituals

This is an important process for successful relations. I am not mentioning here to the use of love spells, as I believe they are unethical. Instead, I am presenting to you a custom of connection that you can count on to focus yourself on your other half regularly. In the end, couples observing traditions and rituals create shared values in life. And this is because daily rituals modify our existence positively.

Just like any aspect is our life, habits are fundamental to success. Overall, they render us healthier and more productive. In relationships, these love habits can help them thrive.

1. Bestowing your partner a brief kiss daily

A daily kiss that lasts for less than a minute will boost your physical and emotional intimacy. Studies revealed that physical contact releases oxytocin, a bonding hormone, which can improve your disposition for days, besides helping you stay serene.

You can also hold hands, hug, touch, whisper little nothings, and make love that trims down cortisol, the stress hormones, as well as increase your feeling of satisfaction in the relationship.

2. Eating meals together devoid of barriers

Away from the cellphone, newspaper, and the broadcasting TV, share your meals with your beloved. Talk about your plans for the day, whatever happened the day before, or your children. During this period, everything else can wait.

3. Having stress-reducing conversations

Each day, spend half an hour to chat with your other half. This can be during mealtimes, but I suggest this be done as an addition to that. The goal of this chat is to talk about external stress and not to take up issues concerning your relationship. Pairs who actively pay attention, take turns revealing their feelings, and show concern to one another will harvest the gifts of more open linking in their bond.

4. Take trips together without the kids

Do this each year to places you both like. If your funds are limited, try looking for reasonably priced accommodations close by for an extended weekend holiday. When you do this regularly, you are also teaching your children the need to maintain the quality of relationships.

5. Working out together

Go hiking together each Saturday late afternoon or enjoy a daily stroll after dinner with your other half. Add a bit of excitement and novelty by trying boating in midsummer or cross skiing in winter. Research has disclosed that having exciting experiences can bring loving pairs closer together.

Never take too lightly the potency of intentional moments with your spouse. Doing fun stuff together like biking or singing can bring laughter and joy. Telling jokes, going to church as a family, watching funny movies, attending parties as a couple, having a body massage together, or anything new can bring you both happiness that ignites passion and keeps you connected.

Raising Unconditional Love

The theory of unconditional affection is a complex one. People hold various beliefs on this topic that ranges from unabashedly taking it to passionately snubbing it. The veracity about unconditional affection is anywhere in between. People who flatly reject the idea of unconditional affection may be looking at it as a too severe definition. They may be thinking of loving someone without boundaries and ignoring themself.

This would entail changing oneself just to continue loving the person irrespective of what that person does to them. So, the beloved can treat them horribly while still being there for that person. If this is your definition of loving unconditionally, then it is unhealthy. Unconditional love denotes that the couple focuses on whatever keeps them together.

It is not ignoring the existence of the relationship and disregarding neglect or abuse. It is not staying together even when both partners exist unhappy. Now, if you are looking to care for your partner unconditionally, you can do it in healthy ways, such as:

1. Working through the rough times.

This means that you both have to endure unfavorable conditions throughout the relationship. You should mutually not let the disappointing and dark times trick you into doubting your bond. Instead, believe with all your hearts that the love you share is worth waging wars for and working through obstacles as one.

2. Believe that both of you deserve happiness.

Actually, this is foremost of all, as one would not ever suggest remaining in a marriage wherein you are displeased. If you really love your partner, you can decide to exert extra effort to work things out. And believing that each of you deserves happiness in life can put you on the right course.

3. Do not surrender at the initial site of failure.

Accept your other half as a human who makes errors as you do. Each of you has obsessions, flaws, opinions, and particularities. After all, even people with the best easy-going attitudes possess quirks. And if your partner is imperfect, this does not mean that he is not suitable for you.

Also, it does not mean that he is a bad person. So, when you understand that nobody is perfect, it really is okay. All you need is to learn effective communication to help both of you work things out.

4. Embrace each moment together.

Keeping Love Alive Long-Term

Loving someone is, foremost of all, a decision. To keep love alive for a lifetime is a matter of will. Love can fade away and die, if not cultivated or intensified. On the other hand, it can grow, blossom, mature, and evolve into a stronger one over time. In long-term relationships that succeed, romantic affection tends to change into companionship.

Romantic love stays increasingly viewed by way of an essential element of matrimony, with 91% of women, besides 86% of men in America, stating that they prefer to marry someone they love even when they may lack the quality they desire in a spouse. This kind of love, left off the hook of the obsessions and craving of the initial phases of loving, frequently remains in long-term relationships.

In fact, some research found that it is correlated with satisfaction in marriage, and individual self-esteem and well-being. Although science gives us some awareness on the description of romantic relationships and love, this fundamental realm of human life remains a mystery. Affection, particularly the enduring kind, has been even considered as among the most researched, but least fathomed, in psychology.

Life-long romance exists, despite great rates of cheating, divorce, and sadness in married life. Scientific research has proven that strong tender love could last a lifespan, besides the published statements of many old couples who have remained in love with their spouses.

Studies even brought forth that carrying on tender love over many years has a helpful function within the brain that knows and lingers to pursue fervent love by way of an action that reaps mental rewards. And these rewards include a decline in stress and fear while boosting the feeling of safety and calmness, as well as accord with another.

MICHELLE MILLER

CHAPTER 30:

Love

Use Affirmations

While displaying love in your marriage, you should also learn the use of affirmations. Affirmations are words or acts that affirm your love for each other. When last did you tell your spouse that you love him or her? When was the last time you bought him a gift to show how you appreciate and love him? Marriage is like a flower that you water every day for it to bloom and grow.

In the same way, you should affirm for each other regularly. It is not enough that your spouse knows that you love him. You should also make him or her feel it. Fortunately, there are more than a thousand ways to express one's love for another. Over the years that you will spend together as a couple, you will definitely not run out of ways to show your love and make your spouse feel it more deeply.

Affirming one's love is done by continuously loving your spouse. There are many ways to affirm your love, whether through your words or deeds. Never forget to tell your spouse that he or she is important to you.

Avoid saying "I love you." as a mere habit. Those are three sacred and powerful words that deserve attention and respect. Say "I love you" because you mean it and say it as you look straight into your beloved's eyes.

Affirming one's love should not be seen as a duty or obligation. After all, if you are truly in love with your spouse, then affirming your love for him or her would be a natural expression of yourself. Also, you will never run out of ways to affirm your love. It can be as easy as cooking his favorite dishes, buying a surprise gift, among many others. It can also be a surprise dinner date at some luxurious restaurant, a special trip for a vacation, etc. There is no boundary to how you can affirm your love for your spouse because love is infinite.

The use of kind words when you give compliments is one of the best ways to express love. When you do this, be sure that you also use the right tone of voice. Words alone are nothing — you also need to be sincere. If you are sincere enough, and if you express your message the right way, then your spouse would feel it.

Affirming your love to your spouse is something that you should continuously do without an end. If you truly love your spouse, then this is something that is very easy and natural to do. People who are in love usually affirm their love even without thinking about it. Unfortunately, during the long course of a marriage and because of the demands of modern life, you may have to remind yourself every now and then to do some positive action to affirm your love to your spouse. This is good, and you should turn this into a habit. Make sure to affirm your love at least once every week.

Make Your Spouse Feel Important

Right now it should be clear to you that your spouse is one of the most important person in the world for you. It is only right that you let him or her know how important he or she is in your life. There are several ways to do this. You can use words and tell him or her just how important he or she is to you and you can also express it through your actions. You can get him a gift, write him a letter, give him a message, or simply treat him in a special way.

If you think that your spouse might not completely understand your kind gesture of love, then use words to make it very clear to him or her. The important thing is to make sure that him or her knows and feels that he or she is important in your life.

When a person is treated in a special way, it makes him feel important. It makes him feel loved. Hence, making your spouse feel important can do wonders for a relationship. Now, if it is your spouse who makes a move to make you feel just how important you are, make sure to express your appreciation. Although this is not related directly to communication, take note that improving the relationship can also improve the level of communication.

Another way to show your spouse just how important he is to you is by listening to him when he talks. A simple example of this is to stop whatever it is that you are doing when he talks to you. Of course, if you are the man, you should also do the same. These days, many couples do not talk properly. It is not uncommon to find couples who talk while the other person is watching a movie or reading a book.

They fail to give 100% of their attention to each other. Yes, you can still engage in conversation and be responsive even while doing something else, but the point here is that you are not giving your spouse your full attention, and this does not make your spouse feel important. You should treat your spouse in a special way.

When you communicate with your spouse, it is always worth reminding yourself that you are talking to the most significant person in your life. Unfortunately, many people fail to realize the value of their spouse and take every moment that they share together for granted. Make every moment count. Focus on your spouse and always treat him or her in a very special way. Now, it is not uncommon for people to feel that they are probably no longer important to their spouse. This is true, especially when your spouse is so busy with work and other obligations that he or she has no time to enjoy life with you — and this is also wrong. Unfortunately, this has become common in many marriages these days. However, you should not let something like this to continue. If you feel like you are in this situation, then you should talk to your spouse about it. Another effective way is to be the one to show to your spouse just how important he is to you. You don't have to make things difficult or suffer in silence. Do not forget that your spouse is there for you. If you are not happy about something in your relationship, then face it together as a team.

It is noteworthy that making your spouse feel important takes positive actions on your part. Do not be content with just knowing that he or she is important to you, but you should communicate this message through your actions and in a way that will make him or her feel just how truly important he or she is in your life.

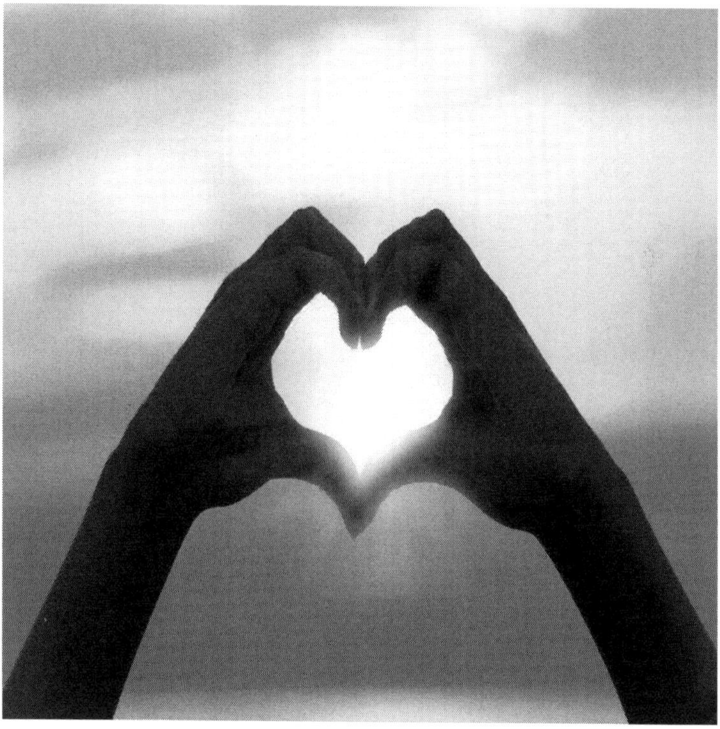

Conclusion

Romantic relationships require hard work; we all know it well. Like cars, they need some regular maintenance to maintain their performance. If a problem happens, it should be fixed immediately to avoid further complications.

We can often do some essential maintenance and repair ourselves. Other times, we have to rely on a specialist to look and to give us a hand, given our efforts.

It is interesting that we take such steps easily and quickly to repair or prevent further damage to our vehicles. But we often avoid acting in our relationships until the situation gets much severe.

Unfortunately, many couples have tried couple therapy when considerable damage has been done already. Maladaptive relationship patterns have become strong, the emotional bonds between partners have severely weakened, and the unresolved past conflicts cause a high level of resentment. The list can continue.

Research supports couples' therapy as an effective way to strengthen their partnership. While there are few reasons to support therapy, many marriage therapy activities help people develop their communication skills, minimize disruptive conduct habits, and enhance their capabilities to be emotionally receptive and attentive to their partners.

If you consider counselling people but don't know if your effort would be worth it, you are not alone. Perhaps you learned about a friend's lack of success or attempted it yourself without much profit.

Good results are more likely when couples who undergo therapy are eager to learn practical skills and become both more self-aware and emotionally insecure. Only fundamental communication skills, such as "feeling" words are required. Most people find it challenging to distinguish between emotions and thoughts. This ability can also be acquired and enhanced during the therapy process.

A second most important feature of successful couples is their ability to avoid treating each other as a foe, but rather as a member of the team, collaborating to enhance mutual happiness, seeing you as "in the same team" increases collaboration and the ability of each person to be emotionally sensitive.

Thirdly, the partner's ability to feel empathy is essential. Every person must have compassion for the feelings of insecurity of others and past emotional traumas.

Finally, the willingness of each person to play their part in the problems and to make a positive change is a prerequisite for successful couples' work. Most people undergo relationship therapy with a list of the other person's grievances and want to see a therapist confirm the grievances and then alter the other person's actions. Although complaints are often valid, nothing can be resolved unless both people are ready to change some element of their conduct.

I hope that the ideas I shared can help you strengthen your relationship with your partner. Expect that there are stormy days in your relationship but facing them together is a sure way to overcome the difficulties. It is significant to have an open line of communication to be able to resolve whatever problems you may encounter in your relationship.

Keep the passion alive and sizzling because it brings pleasure and happiness. Cultivate the relationship with love, trust and commitment. It will steer you away from temptations, heartaches and tears. Make it a habit to rekindle your passion every day by showing how much you mean to each other.

Remember that it always takes two persons to build a relationship and also two to make it lasts. It is in your hands.

If you enjoyed this guide, take the time to share your thoughts and post a review. It'd be greatly appreciated!

Thank you and good luck!

If you've enjoyed this book , then you can also read "Anxiety in relationship" from the same author Michelle Miller

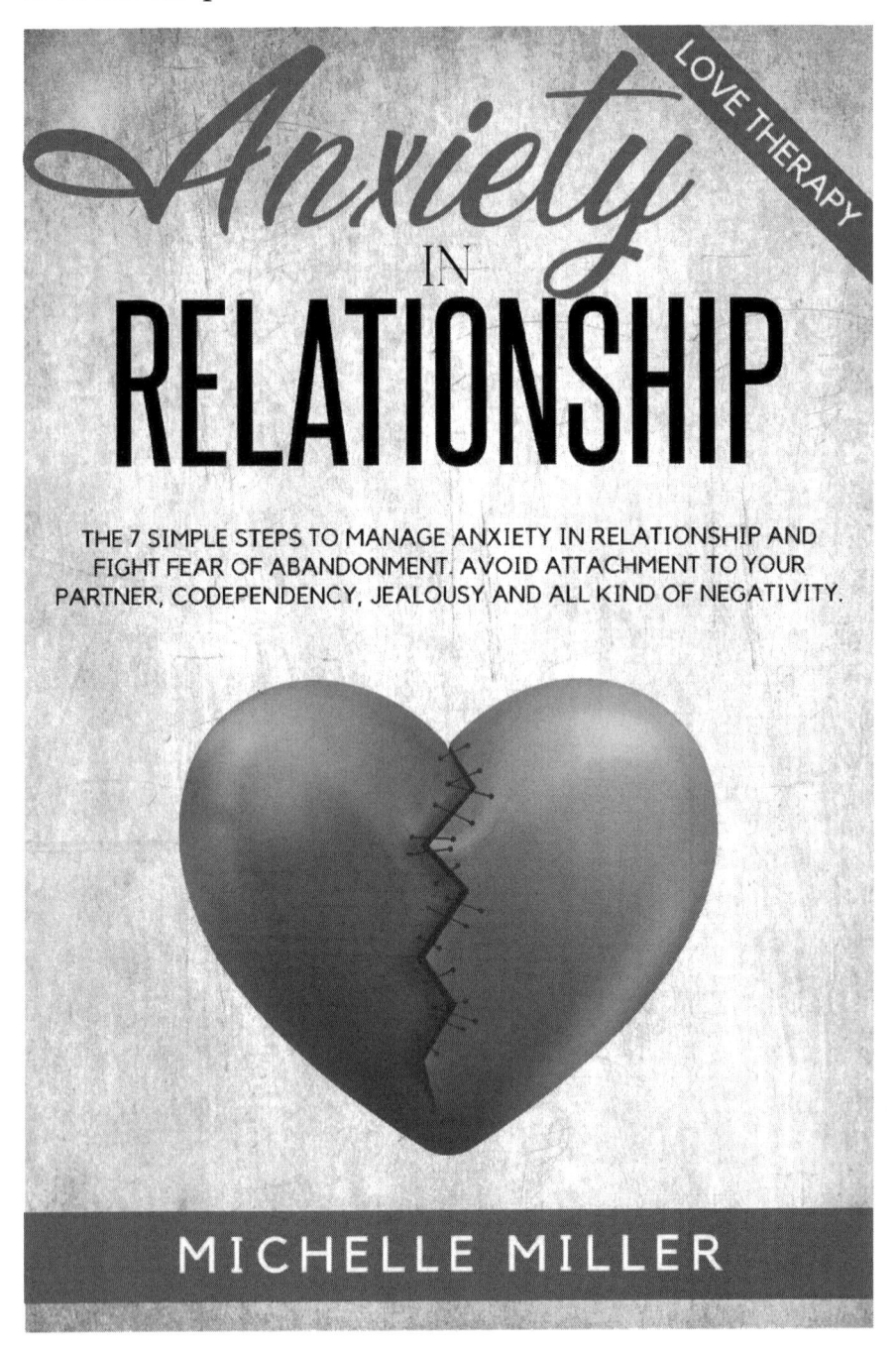

Printed in Great Britain
by Amazon